SACRED
CONNECTIONS

STORIES OF ADOPTION

Essays by Mary Ann Koenig

Photographs by Niki Berg

Running Press
PHILADELPHIA • LONDON

Essays © 2000 by Mary Ann Koenig
Photographs © 2000 by Niki Berg

9   8   7   6   5   4   3   2   1
Digit on the right indicates the number of this printing

Library of Congress Cataloging-in-Publication Number 00-131323

ISBN 0-7624-0801-4

Edited by Carol Schaefer
Designed by Mary Ann Liquori
Typography: Fairfield

This book may be ordered by mail from the publisher. Please include $2.50 for postage and handling.
But try your bookstore first!

Running Press Book Publishers
125 South Twenty-second Street
Philadelphia, Pennsylvania 19103-4399

Visit us on the web!
www.runningpress.com

For my sons, Matthew and Ben—for the joy of holding you close and seeing you grow.

—Mary Ann Koenig

For my daughters, Jessica, Karina, and Emily, who in their own unique way have enriched my life beyond measure.

—Niki Berg

CONTENTS

FOREWORD

SACRED CONNECTIONS. THEY ARE THAT. THE ADOPTEES, birth parents, and adoptive parents in this book give vision and voice to the reality of families made by adoption. Having worked with this population for thirty years as a family therapist and psychologist, I have had the honor and opportunity to witness the natural progression of families who open up and accept all that is good for them (and especially good for their children). As a clinician and trainer, I believe stories are an integral part of the healing process. The telling and retelling of our stories empower the storyteller to hold his or her own story—and, consequently, his or her own life—sacred.

SACRED CONNECTIONS. THAT THEY ARE! THIS BOOK IS a source of honor, respect, love, and joy, and it will help the rest of the world to understand what many already know: Families are extended and loving. Having more than one mother, more than one father, and more than one set of siblings does not confuse who your parents are. It simply validates who your whole family is.

Blessed be the families of adoption that can open up and accept each other with love and respect.

Blessed be the child who is loved by many.

Dr. Joyce Maguire Pavao
May, 2000

When I was young, I loved feeling that I was special. After all, most parents had to take what they got, but my adoptive parents chose me over all of the other available babies. By the time I was seven years old, however, another thought occurred to me: in order for me to be chosen, didn't someone have to let me go? I remember asking all sorts of questions about my first mother: "Who was she?" "What color was her hair?" "Why couldn't she keep me?" With every question, I saw a look on my mother's face that I'd never seen before. Maybe fear, maybe hurt.

Neither the doctor and attorney nor the social worker prepared my mother to expect these questions. She believed that telling me I was loved and special would be enough to carry me through adolescence and adulthood. She didn't have accurate information about my birth parents. My mother backed away from my questions, and her retreat sent an unspoken message: "This is painful—you certainly don't want to hurt your mother or risk losing her, so don't bring it up."

One day in school, a classmate, tired of hearing about my "special" status, said, "Not only are you not so special, but your real mom didn't want you." I was devastated. Part of me already knew this was true, and now everyone knew.

The story of how I came into the world became infused with shame, mystery, and power—it was without question a dangerous topic. My mother was afraid of it, and so was I.

I was adopted into a closed adoption in 1948. Closed adoption is an adoption in which the original birth certificate is amended to read as if the child were born into the adoptive family. My original birth certificate and adoption records were closed by the court.

Prior to World War II, most states did not seal off the original birth certificates of adoptees. Although this information was kept away from public scrutiny, the birth and adoptive families still had access to these records. By the late forties and fifties, however, individual states were sealing off their adoption records. This was in part due to the stigma of "illegitimacy." The social and legal solution was to seal off the original birth certificate and record of adoption, and issue an amended birth certificate as if the child was born to his/her adoptive parents. What started out as a matter of privacy—to protect the privacy of the child, birth, and adoptive families from public scrutiny—was transformed into a matter of secrecy. Those who were adopted, even as adults, would have no access to their original birth certificates or adoption records. Although this solution ensured a permanent home for children, it did not address the impact of life-long secrecy. No one seemed to consider that teenage birth mothers would grow into mature women. No one anticipated that adopted children would grow up and have questions about their backgrounds. Few understood that many birth mothers, rather than "moving on with their lives" once the pregnancy and birth was behind them, were stuck for years in a state of numbness; if and when the numbness lifted, the mothers experienced a flood of sadness and a yearning to know about the well-being of their child. It was a solution that exchanged the mark of "illegitimacy" for the mark of secrecy.

It is natural for children to want to know who gave them life. When adoptive parents believe this and are given all available, accurate information about their child's history, they are in a better position to act as guides along a path toward understanding. Telling a child of his adoption is not a singular event—it is an experience that evolves over time, as important to the entire family as it is to the adoptee. When parents embrace the known and even the unknown aspects of their child's history and make it part of the family history, it creates an environment in which the growing child is free to experience a full gamut of feelings, ask questions, and integrate slowly what it means to be adopted. When the parents are free to discuss it, so is the child.

NIKI BERG AND I HAVE SPENT MORE THAN TWO YEARS researching and interviewing subjects for this book, and it has been an incredible journey. We were touched by the lives of each person in this book. They welcomed us into their homes, fed us wonderful food, and shared their most intimate memories. We cried together, laughed together, and gathered so many treasured memories along the way.

While spending time with seventy-three year-old old Jim Rockwell, we went in search of the famous Petoskey stone, a honeycomb-patterned fossil that washes up on the lake beaches in that one area of Michigan. Niki, Jim, and I were perched at the top of a huge sand dune that sloped sharply toward the beach. We looked at each other, shrugged, and said, "What the hell." Niki led the way, Jim brought up the rear, and we all took baby steps sideways down the dune. Control was the key. But then Jim caught his foot on a ground root and became airborne. In a slow motion ballet, he collided into me, and the two of us gathered up Niki into a human ball, rolling head over feet to the bottom. There was no harm done. And we laughed and laughed.

Niki and I had the good fortune of interviewing Barrie Shibley during the 1999 Calgary Stampede. Every year in July, all of the business in Calgary comes screeching to a halt. Men and women don cowboy hats, jeans, and pointed toe boots, and let loose for ten days of partying. Barrie and his business partner, John, managed to get great seats in the grand stand for us to see young cowboys hanging on for their lives as bucking bulls tried to send them flying. Barrie and John also requested special permission for us to stand, ground level, at an entrance gate to watch a few events. No one had expected so much rain in the days leading up to the stampede, so there was thick mud everywhere. In most places, wooden planks were placed on the ground so people could walk mud-free from one place to the next. But there were no wooden planks leading up to the special entrance gate, where we would have the privilege of watching cowboys roping steers, up close and personal. I looked down at my brand new, suede, open-toed sandals. It's hard to describe the sound and sensation of sinking ankle deep in a combination of mud and bull dung—I'll just say it was one of the high points of our journey.

Finally, in December 1999, we traveled to Saskatchewan,

Canada to interview a First Nation Ojibiway adoptee, Sharon Jinkerson. During our visit, Sharon and her Auntie Grace invited us to participate in a sweat. The weather was near zero (and felt even colder with the wind chill). A major snow storm was on the way.

When we arrived, women were standing around a fire in a teepee and changing into lightweight nightgowns. Niki and I brought gifts of broadcloth and tobacco for the elders who ran the sweat. We also brought two towels—one to sit on, and one to hold up to our faces to protect us from the heat. Sharon explained that if I needed to leave, I should say out loud "All my relations," and the chief elder would arrange to have the flap of the sweat lodge opened.

The elders were gathered inside the sweat—a low, igloo shaped structure. Men and women outside the sweat were tending the rocks, making sure they were red hot. I followed Niki, Sharon, and Grace into the opening on my hands and knees. Sharon wanted me to sit by her, but it was crowded and I instinctively knew I needed to be by the flap opening. Men and women sat in a circle around a shallow pit of rocks at the center. Bear grease was passed to rub on places on the body where we felt physical or spiritual pain.

The sweat has many symbols—nine rocks in the center pit represent each month of gestation. The bowl of the pipe symbolizes the womb and the stem is the life force. When the two are joined, life is created. Walter, the chief elder, asked that the door keeper close the flap. We were entombed in total blackness. As the elders led prayers and chanted, herbed water was thrown on the burning rocks. Hot steam—hotter than anything I'd ever experienced—hit my face. I couldn't breathe.

I wrapped my towel around my head, but I felt like I was suffocating. I didn't want to say "All my relations." I didn't want to be the one to disrupt the ceremony. But my fear was escalating. I tried to talk myself down from the panic, but I couldn't. "Sharon, all my relations," I said. Sharon told the chief I was having difficulty and needed the flap opened. He asked me if I had my towel to my face. "Yes, but it's not working," I replied. He told me to press my nose to the ground. Part of me wanted to scream, "Just let me out!" Instead, I shifted my body, and put my nose to the ground. The floor was covered with thin carpeting, except for one small rectangle by the door flap—it was covered with ice, my connection to the outside world.

I pressed my nose to the patch of ice and pushed my head against the closed flap. My bottom was in the air. Walter, the chief elder, asked everyone to pray for me, to call on the ancestors to help me. A rhythmic, soothing chanting filled the air. One woman rubbed my back. Another woman pressed points on my foot with her fingertips. Slowly, my panic lessened. But I remained for the rest of the round with my bottom in the air, my nose pressed to the ice, and my head pushed against the opening. Confining. Dark. Hot. Damp. Frightening. Soothing. Rhythmic prayers. The chief elder, Walter, asked the doorkeeper to open the flap. As he did, my head pushed through and I landed on the snow-covered ground.

THE INDIVIDUALS AND FAMILIES IN *SACRED CONNections* attest to the struggle, courage, tenderness, and humor of adoptees, birth parents, and adoptive parents in their effort to create meaning of their adoption experience. These are inspiring and liberating stories that demonstrate those moments in all of our lives when we keep our hearts and minds open, embrace our fears, and create a richer, more inclusive and joyous life.

THIS PROJECT CAME TO ME IN THE MOST SERENDIPITOUS way. By chance, I met a woman in California who had a friend, Mary Ann, in need of a photographer for a book on adoption. Might be interesting, I thought, since I'm a portrait photographer and have always been interested in family dynamics. I met Mary Ann and with eagerness we agreed to work together.

It wasn't until well into the project that I recognized my own complicated history and feelings regarding this sacred connection. In the process of the work, I came face to face with my unconscious and profound personal involvement.

I am married to Peter and the mother of a triad of daughters: Jessica my step-daughter, Karina my daughter by birth, and Emily, the daughter I never met, who died in my womb during labor. Oddly enough, I know the adoptive story from three sides: the miracle of birthing a child, the pain of losing a child, and the complex feelings around raising a child I didn't birth.

The first time I met a birth mother, I identified so deeply with her loss I could barely speak. Suddenly, I found myself thinking about Emily, the tiny infant girl who was whisked away from me in the delivery room before I even had a chance

to see what she looked like. It didn't occur to the doctor, Peter, or me to take a few moments to let me hold my child and say goodbye. Those few moments would have provided some closure to the intimate "relationship" Emily and I had experienced during the nine months that I carried her.

I felt like such a failure—to my two girls, to my husband, and especially to my new stillborn daughter. I now realize that I was in a state of shock for many years, unable or unwilling to delve into my feelings about what had happened. It has taken me years to recognize and release the resentment and pain around this tragedy.

For a long time I was unable to speak Emily's name without tears. Now when I think of Emily, I smile with gratitude. She taught me invaluable lessons about life and loss.

Jessica came into my life when she was eight, when I married her father. Her mother Rhoda had died three years earlier. Legally, there was no need for formal adoption. Emotionally, becoming a mother overnight was overwhelming. I felt tremendous love for her alongside paralyzing fear of my new responsibility. It began a process, a constant ebbing and flowing,

10

from fear to faith, to fear again, and at last into that confident place of mother.

While working on the book, I decided with much excitement to adopt Jessica legally. Sadly, I found myself thwarted. The New York State adoption laws require that Jessica's original birth certificate be sealed and a new one issued naming me as her mother as though I had birthed her. The idea of erasing Rhoda's identity from Jessica's history was intolerable. We have decided, after thirty years of a mother/daughter relationship, to make this adoption official in our own personal way.

In the early days of motherhood, I had a hard time accepting the differences in my relationships with Karina and Jessica. I have since come to understand that each child in a family has his or her own separate and unique place in the heart of the mother, regardless of the original connection.

During the course of the two year journey to create *Sacred Connections* I have been awakened to the challenge of integrating and balancing my feelings about my three children. Through this exploration, I have gained wisdom, consciousness, and a new sense of peace. My gratitude and admiration goes out to all the people involved in the process of adoption, the families in this book for their willingness to share their stories, and to all the families around the world who are courageously working to piece together an open and loving family union.

Niki Berg
May, 2000

Susan at home in Eugene, Oregon

SUSAN SOON-KEUM COX

MEMORIES OF SUSAN'S EARLY CHILDHOOD IN KOREA WOULD COME TO HER in fragments: "I am four years old and I am sitting across the room from a woman holding a baby. Next to me is a dark-skinned man. He is angry. I look down and see a knife pointed at my stomach. I am looking at the woman, imploring her to look at me. She doesn't look at me because she will cry. The woman is my mother.

"I am walking along quickly. A woman is holding my hand. I don't know where I am going, but somehow I have the sense that I am never coming back. We walk into this place and I am overwhelmed by the noise of all the children. I am frightened because I don't know what I am supposed to do. But I try very hard not to cry."

Looking back, Susan remembers, "My brown hair was dyed black before I was taken to the orphanage. I have felt proud of that gesture, as it was an indication of how someone tried to keep me looking pure Korean, and therefore more acceptable, though my father was not Korean."

Susan's memories were her secret as she grew up with her adoptive parents in the small rural community of Brownsville, Oregon. "When I was little, I dreamed my mother was a princess, a young and beautiful woman who fell in love with my father, a wonderful and handsome soldier. In my imagination, I was never quite able to resolve what happened or what went wrong. I just knew they loved each other, and something terrible must have happened to keep them from being together. By the time my Korean mother gave birth to me, my father had already left the 'Land of the Morning Calm.'"

Over the years, Susan was able to let go of wondering about her mother. Yet she could not let go of the desire to know who she looked like. The birth of her first child offered her the opportunity to gaze at someone who mirrored her appearance. "My baby was born three weeks late. As they took my beautiful son to be washed and dressed, I lay alone in the recovery room, unbelievably happy, but with mixed emotions as I remembered my birth mother. I thought of this generation beginning thousands of miles from its origins."

Susan's first visitor in the hospital was her grandmother, her adoptive father's mother. "I heard her voice in the hallway outside the nursery before I saw her: 'See that baby there? The boy with all the hair? That's my great-grandson.' The pride and joy in her voice made my eyes fill with tears. She held my son with competence, folding back the blanket to reveal his naked little body for her inspection. She touched him tenderly all over, pulled the soft blanket around him, and said to me, 'Susie, he looks exactly like your father, especially his ears. He definitely has his grandpa's ears.' To me this was my 'real' grandmother, not adoptive, talking about my 'real' father and my 'real' son. At that moment there was no room to think about anyone else."

Susan's son was nearly two when her adoptive father died. She was twenty-six. "I always dreaded this horrible moment. I drove to my parents' farm, crying the whole way. I kept thinking, 'I am only one parent away from being an orphan again.' My feelings of grief and loss for my father were matched by my terror for myself."

Two years after her father died, Susan gave birth to a daughter, Katee. When Katee turned four, she began asking questions about Susan's birth mother.

"They were important questions. It seemed significant that she began to wonder about her mother's beginnings at the same age when much of that happened to me."

In 1979, Susan finally returned to Korea with her husband. "The trip was exciting and terrifying. Friends repeatedly asked, 'Will you look for your real mom?' But it didn't interest me. My interest was to rediscover the country of my birth and share it with my husband. While I didn't realize it at the time, that trip marked the beginning of my search."

Susan began looking for her birth mother in earnest in 1992, as she approached her fortieth birthday. She also marked this milestone by reclaiming her Korean name, Soon Keum, meaning "pure gold." As she contemplated the search, she remembered what it was like to be left at the orphanage as a little girl. "I remember wanting my mother so much. I wanted to feel her arms around me. I wanted to smell her, feel her breath. She knew I was afraid of the dark. I thought, surely this was a mistake. She would never let me be hungry like this. We had never been away from each other for so long. I was so scared. Surely she was coming soon to bring me home."

Susan needed to know if her mother's spirit, dreams, and visions were the same as her own. She needed to know if her mother sent powerful thoughts to her over the years. "Or am I this person simply because I am, and therefore unconnected to anything I received from being her daughter?" she wondered.

In 1992, she placed an ad in the Inchon Newspaper in Korea, with a plea for information about her birth mother. Four months later, she received a fax from a social worker, Mrs. Choi. It read: 'Your birth mother Chung Kwan Ja died September, 1979.'

"My mother died the year I first visited Korea," Susan says. She learned she had two half brothers and wrote to them. After receiving her first letter, the oldest brother wrote: "My mother passed away fourteen years ago and the father fell back to the dust three years ago, too. When the mother was standing in the presence of death, she told me I have an elder sister in America. I was reminded of the mother's appearance occasionally and she just kept everything about you in her heart alone. And even she couldn't talk to me, who was her son. I try to understand mother's heart now. The mother was born in regrettable world and led a life full of tears and sadness. I was undutiful son to mother. Please forgive me. If mother were alive now, she would be very pleased to hear from you."

Her youngest brother wrote, too: "When I looked at mother, she seemed to be anxious about something always. Sometimes she looked at the sky and sighed as if she had a big worry. We did not know the source of sadness in our mother's life."

Susan's brothers had a different father than her own. "Their father was Korean. When I looked at photographs they sent of my mother and their father, I thought I recognized the dark-skinned man and wondered if it was he who had held the knife to my stomach when I was four." In the photo of her mother, Susan did not see the image she had expected, of the young woman frozen in time. What she saw was an old woman, with strength and dignity and a face that had lived a hard, sad life. "I was surprised at how much I resembled her. It was our mouths that looked so similar. My daughter has the same mouth, so for three generations it has continued."

Soon after receiving her brothers' letters, Susan returned to Korea to meet her birth family. "There was a crowd of people at the airport, but I had no trouble spotting my brothers. When they greeted me, they held me close with tears streaming down their cheeks. The older brother took my hand, looked at my lifeline, and compared it to his. 'Very good,' he said."

Toward the end of her visit, Susan went with her brothers to the cemetery where their mother was buried. She stood above the grave, a tangled mass of weeds. "This final resting place was an accurate illustration of her life. No one ever tended her garden. In her whole life, no one nurtured her, cared for her, made her safe. Including me."

"The ritual at our mother's grave was strange and unfamiliar to me," Susan remembers. "Yet at the same time, it was comforting. One brother said to me, 'You are the eldest, you go first.' It was true, I was born first. But I was new to this. I did not know how to lead this ritual of respect and honor. 'You go first.' The words were spoken again, and my two brothers stepped back, motioning me toward our mother's grave. I

stepped in front of the mound of earth that came nearly to my shoulders and was covered with stiff grass. Even the burial place of my mother was foreign.

"My brothers told me to bow four times. I bowed stiffly. 'Like this?' I asked. They nodded. I bowed again, three times, more aware of them than of the spirit of our mother. The second born, then the third born, bowed reverently. They had done this many times before. I realized I did not bow properly. They knelt in front of the grave together, and I echoed them."

Without words, they passed pieces of dried fish among themselves. After placing the remaining fish on the grave, the brothers nodded to Susan that it was time to chew. "I did everything like them, exactly. I felt like a shadow. Still without words, they poured rice wine into three glasses for us and one glass for our mother. They handed her glass to me to place gently on the grave. We drank together, and were silent. The only noise was the grass waving softly in the cemetery. I looked out over the rice fields that surrounded my mother's final resting place. Then I raised my glass to my brothers and said, 'To our mother, Chung Kwan Ja. I am sure this would make her happy. . . the three of us together.'"

Her brothers shook their heads vigorously. "'No, no! Not Chung Kwan Ja. *Chung Kwan Ja*. You are not saying it correctly.' As if they were speaking to a child, they put their faces close to mine and repeated our mother's name slowly. I repeated it back to them. 'No, no, still wrong,' they told me. We went back and forth until I got it right or they gave up on me. At first I was hurt, and then it passed. I did say it wrong. It is because I did not have her to show me. I did not hear my mother's name every day as they did.

"But now I was with them, and with her. I reached for my brothers' hands and prayed silently, prayers that were sad, thoughtful, and happy, all at once. 'I was always your secret,' I whispered to her. 'It is not necessary anymore. I will find the right words to tell our story. I promise you.'"

THE ONLY RECOGNITION OF ANY KIND THAT THIRTEEN YEAR-OLD JENNIFER Huntsberry received after the birth of her son came from the social worker at the adoption agency. "She sent me a bouquet of flowers with a toy giraffe tucked into it. The card didn't say, 'God bless you.' It didn't say, 'God bless your baby.' It said, 'God bless your decision.'"

Following the delivery, Jennifer was moved into an area of women recovering from hysterectomies and other gynecological procedures. "I was put in a private room, away from the maternity ward, so I wouldn't have to endure the other mothers' happiness. Knowing their babies were visiting made me very lonesome," she recalls. The social worker had advised Jennifer not to see her baby, so she wouldn't get attached to him. Everyone was giving her the same advice. "Since so many people were saying the same thing, I figured it must be true. And I knew all along that I couldn't keep my child. I was a thirteen year-old child myself. I was not capable of being a parent.

"During my pregnancy, I was never depressed when I thought about the baby—only scared about all the huge decisions I was making that would affect both of us the rest of our lives. I prayed to God to please help me face the situation and make mature decisions. When I was alone and felt my child move inside me, felt a little knee or elbow push, I could feel God surrounding me with warmth and love.

"I held my son when he was born, and marveled at his perfection. After his birth, my maternal feelings were overwhelming. I wanted to give him the world, but all I had to offer was my love."

nifer, birth mother, and Aaron, birth son, visiting in the family apple orchard (Beulah, Michigan)

After leaving the hospital, Jennifer returned to the maternity home where she lived during the final months of her pregnancy. The arrival of her baby had put an extra strain on an already difficult relationship with her family, and she preferred the maternity home, where she received support and guidance, both before and after the birth. The home even assigned Jennifer a foster mother of her own.

"When my baby was a week old, the adoption was going forward, but I realized it was going forward without me," Jennifer says. "I decided I wanted more involvement with my son than just occasional pictures. I wanted to get to know the adopting parents that the agency had selected." A meeting was set up with the social worker, but at the last minute, Jennifer could not make herself go. "I suddenly felt that I was dealing with too many important decisions all at once, while having to recover physically as well. I needed time to clear my mind, so I could be certain about my plans."

with my foster mother. In the middle of the store, my milk suddenly came in. My clothes were sopping wet. Milk was dripping down the front of my shirt. I had refused to take pills to dry it up, because I wanted to experience what it was like to have the ability to breastfeed, even though I wasn't going to." A woman from her foster mother's church told her about Jim Gritter, a social worker whose adoption agency in Traverse City offered fully open adoptions.

The fact that he made the five-hour trip to her home twice convinced Jennifer that Jim Gritter had her best interests in mind, as well as those of his clients. The first time, he brought a trunkload of profiles of prospective adoptive parents. On his second visit, he brought a married couple, Cameron and Jane, and their first adoptive son, Garrett. They had been Jennifer's first choice after reading the profiles, and she found their effort to meet her reassuring.

Cameron and Jane admit that when they first went through

"IT WAS EXTREMELY PAINFUL TO LET HIM GO. IT TOOK A WHOLE YEAR FOR ME TO MAKE A FINAL RELEASE, TO FULLY REALIZE HE WAS IN GOOD HANDS."

Another meeting with the adopting parents was set for a week later. "The social worker told me the man said I needed to get my act together and keep that next appointment, because he and his wife couldn't take off another day of work. I realized that if they felt that way toward me now, I would always be treated as an obligation, a hoop they had to jump through in order to get my baby. Obviously, their promise to send me pictures of him every three months was solely for my benefit. Not for the child. Not for themselves. They wanted the baby and I was something they had to deal with. I knew I couldn't sign the papers, because once I did, I'd have no legal recourse. No matter how much they promised, they were under no obligation to follow through with anything. I just couldn't release my son to this agency, in this situation, to this couple."

But the administrators at the maternity home didn't offer Jennifer any alternatives. "A few days later, I went shopping

the adoption process with Garrett, they were focused entirely on their own needs. Birth mothers were faceless people in the background—not like any people they would ever know. But as they gradually got used to the idea of open adoption and met a few birth mothers, they gained a new perspective. They realized open adoption could be a beautiful, even spiritual, experience.

"What impressed me most about Cameron and Jane is that they were both very open to developing a true and continuing relationship with me," Jennifer says. "They were offering friendship, not just sharing the information that was required to adopt my child. Also, they were both teachers. And I was glad to learn that they lived on a farm with beautiful orchards that Jane's family had tended for generations.

"During our first visit, Jane sat in the middle of our living room floor while Garrett crawled all over her. Finally, he crawled into her lap and fell asleep. She rocked him the whole time." Once Jennifer had finalized her decision to place the baby with them, she spent some time alone with him. "I picked him up at the foster home and took him home with me for four days. It was important for me to hold him, take care of him, get to know him. I didn't get that opportunity in the hospital or in the foster home. My Mom went to work and my stepdad was away, so it was just me and the baby. The work of caring for him didn't matter. It was a time of cherishing him. All I did was hold him and look at him. I didn't even turn on the TV. He cried when I gave him a bath. It was hard to hear him cry."

Her son was a month old when she finally brought him to Cameron and Jane. "He needed to be with them as soon as possible," Jennifer says. "He'd already been cared for by too many people." She and Cameron and Jane spent most of the day together, getting to know each other. While the baby slept on Jennifer's chest, they agreed on what to name him. Aaron was her choice. His middle name, Alex, was Cameron and Jane's. This collaborative naming process, they felt, represented how they could all work together to do what was best for the child.

"Leaving him took so long," Jennifer recalls. "I said good-bye so many times. At first I held him. Then I handed him to Jane. We said good-bye in the living room, then in the kitchen. Then we moved to the foyer. Finally, we just had to go. I was crying so hard. My mom didn't say much. My brother was driving and I was in the back seat, immersed in pain. All the way home, I pretended to be asleep."

Before she left that day, Cameron and Jane gave Jennifer a necklace with a verse from Genesis engraved on it: "The Lord watch between me and thee while we are apart from one another." The heart pendant is broken in two. Jennifer has one half, and Aaron has the other. They also gave her a letter which, she believes, sets the tone for their entire relationship.

Dear Jennifer,

As you return home, we cannot begin to realize how you feel leaving your son behind. It is a strange situation that your unhappiness should become our joy. We can only assure you that he is going to be loved a lot and thought of as very special. Through our inability to give birth, we know only too well how precious children are. We are sure you are anticipating the next time we contact you. It will be soon. We already have the camera loaded and ready. Remember, don't feel uneasy about initiating contact with us. You are part of us now. We will always be interested in hearing from you and seeing you. The enclosed medallion is something for you and the baby to share always. We are mounting his half in a small frame and as he begins to understand, he will know that the other half is with you, his birth mom, who loves and cares for him deeply. We hope and pray as time passes God will give you peace of mind and much happiness.

Love,

Cameron and Jane

The first year that Jennifer visited them, saying good-bye was always long and difficult. Sometimes it took an hour. In the beginning, there was no set plan, but they gradually settled into a routine of monthly visits. Since Jennifer was too young to drive, Cameron and Jane sent bus tickets, or one of Jennifer's siblings would drive her to spend the weekend. On occasion, Cameron and Jane visited her family.

"Nothing was going to take the pain away but seeing him—and time," Jennifer says. "Holding him and loving him helped me deal with my sadness. It was extremely painful to let him go. It took a whole year for me to make a final release, to fully realize he was in good hands. Even after that, it still hurt."

When Aaron was a toddler, Jennifer frequently took him bicycling. It became one of their most important activities together. "Jane lent me her bike with the baby seat on it," Jennifer recalls. "Aaron and I would ride into town. We'd buy an ice cream cone, stop by the five and ten cent store, then go feed the ducks at Crystal Lake. Jane always gave us a bag of bread. Then we'd walk out on the pier to watch the fish. Jane

From left: Aaron, Cameron, Megan, Jane, Garrett, and Jennifer (holding Emily)

encouraged us to have time alone, without anyone hovering, so we could get to know each other. I needed to have my private talks with Aaron. I was very proud of him. He always knew I was Jenny, his birth mom."

In the years to come, Cameron and Jane would play a major role in Jennifer's life. When Aaron was three and a half, Jennifer graduated from high school. After she got engaged to Chris, they bought her wedding gown. Jennifer began college, and then gave birth to Megan. She went on to complete pharmacy school, and she and Chris had a second daughter, Emily. Cameron, Jane, Garrett, and Aaron participated in all of Jennifer's celebrations. They were truly a part of her family.

"For many years, there was a lot going on with my life," Jennifer reflects. "As the years passed, we saw each other less often. Right around Aaron's tenth birthday, I called to make plans to visit. During our conversation, Jane said to me, 'Aaron

needs you. He needs you.' I felt guilty. I hadn't realized how important I was to him. Aaron told Jane that he felt bad because he didn't know if he was as important to me as he used to be. This relationship was actually as much for him as it was for me."

The familial connection continues to evolve. Cameron and Jane know their sons will have issues to deal with, but secrecy will not be one of them. They believe that when children are told the truth, the answers to any questions they ask are simple, and that Aaron should feel he is a part of both families. After Megan asked, "Who is Aaron?", he gained his rightful place in her family because Jennifer told her eldest daughter the truth.

In Jane's family's orchards, branches carry the burden of ripened fruit. Jennifer knows that whatever the season, whatever the harvest—apples, cherries, or apricots—her family is always welcome to take a bucket and pick a bushel.

SHERRY BABB

EMILY YANG XIN BABB

THROUGH CHINA'S HARSH WINTER MONTHS, LITTLE EMILY WAS NURSED BY her birth mother, until warmer weather ensured that she could survive being left by the side of a road.

In rural China, most families hope for a son to help with the farm, to care for them in their old age, and to carry on the family name. The government policy of allowing one child per family means that baby girls are often abandoned. The consequences of abandoning a child include losing jobs, land rights, property, and insurance, yet China's orphanages still have an abnormally high percentage of baby girls.

Reading about their plight touched Sherry Babb's heart. "I wanted to rescue every last one of them," she remembers. After a few of her friends adopted daughters from China, Sherry began to consider the idea more closely. "Their babies had such sweet temperaments. The little girls were alert and engaged, connected to life. I couldn't stand knowing that they were considered nonentities in their own country, that they had so little value or opportunity."

The decision to adopt was a long process for Sherry. "Relationships weren't cutting it for me. I considered finding a sperm donor, but finally decided that, in order to keep my job and career afloat, I could not afford the down time of pregnancy all by myself. Adoption seemed the way to go."

Adopting a baby from China required a great deal of paperwork and money. To help accumulate the necessary funds, one friend gave Sherry a second loan on her house.

Other friends threw a fund-raiser to help raise more cash. "I kept records of everything," Sherry explains. "When Emily gets older, I want her to know everyone who contributed their energy to bring her here."

When it came time for Sherry to meet her adoptive daughter, she was joined by her cousin Pam. They flew to a rural steel town, Wuhan, on the Yangtse River in northeastern China. "When we arrived at the hotel, we were jet-lagged beyond repair," she recalls. "My cousin and I fell on the beds exhausted, still fully clothed, expecting to get the baby after a good rest. We were in the deepest, deadest, darkest sleep when the phone rang. We were asked to be down in the lobby in twenty minutes. The most exciting time of my life was about to take place, and I was in no way prepared for it.

"Pam and I scrambled to gather the presents we had brought for the foster family, the doctor, the guide, and various other people. We'd brought lipstick, toiletries, candy, and T-shirts. My family had given me a camcorder to film everyone, but I didn't have a clue how to use it."

Sherry and Pam rushed down to the hotel's conference room and met nine other sets of adoptive parents. "We all looked like exhausted deer caught in the headlights, frozen in a state of anticipation," Sherry recalls. The babies were brought into the room, one at a time, by caregivers or foster families. Each adopting family already knew what their child looked like from photographs received at Christmas. "In her photo, Emily had a little red bindi on her forehead—a mark that Buddhists put on children they consider very special. She was as cute as could be."

The first family to receive their baby began to weep. The caregiver from the orphanage followed suit, and the baby cried uncontrollably. It was clear that the caregivers and foster families had all grown attached to the little girls.

"Finally, every single one of us burst into tears. It was like the dam just broke," Sherry recalls. "It was heartbreaking to watch child after child taken from the care providers and fos-

ter families, and placed in the hands of total strangers who looked alarmingly unlike anyone they'd ever seen. The children were screaming and crying. I remember thinking there couldn't be anything more emotional in life than this. Nothing can be more traumatic than being wrenched from all you've known. I began to feel unsure about what I was doing with this little girl."

Pam operated the video camera as Emily's foster mother brought in a fourteen-month-old girl. "Emily was crying," Sherry remembers. "Her foster mother, on the other hand, was smiling and patting Emily. She didn't speak a word of English, so it was a quick transition. She showed the translator that Emily wore a heart-shaped necklace inscribed with her nickname, Xin Xin (pronounced Sheen-Sheen). Then she turned and walked out.

The adopting families began asking Pam to videotape them. Suddenly Emily's foster mother returned, crying uncontrollably. She didn't want to leave. Her crying just seemed to make Emily more upset.

"I was so overwhelmed," Sherry recalls. "Everything was surreal. That is the only word I can use. I had this child in my arms—my child, who didn't want anything to do with me. She was screaming and I couldn't console her. The whole room was filled with babies we couldn't console. These were cries of utter heartbreak."

Emily sobbed almost continuously for a week. "My child's heart was shattered. She wailed 'Mama' for so long. She would clutch the little heart necklace and just bawl. After the first three days, we removed the necklace while she was sleeping," Sherry says. "It was better, but she still cried for Mama, and she wouldn't take a bottle. We couldn't get her to eat or drink. Every time we left the hotel room, she'd get really excited and start screaming, 'Mama! Mama!' She thought we were taking her to see her Mama."

Culture shock made the entire adoption process more difficult. The people in China seemed puzzled when they saw

Emily and Sherry in their garden (Sag Harbor, New York)

Americans holding Chinese babies, until the agency printed up a flier, which explained that the grateful Americans had come to adopt baby girls. "Once they read the flier, people started smiling and blessing us. Because I'm blond, I attracted a lot of attention. People touched my hair. Behind my back, they took pictures of it. It was overwhelming."

After a week of this, Sherry thought that taking Emily might be a mistake. "I remember thinking, 'I don't care how poor these people are—separating these children from people who have loved them is wrong.' But one of the doctors said to me, 'You're forgetting something, Sherry. They can't keep the children, even if they wanted to.' Understanding that made me feel better."

After the first week, the situation began to improve. "We were able to get Emily to smile a little bit," Sherry says. "It worked better if we held her facing out, instead of looking directly at us, especially when we fed her. We called me 'Mommy' now and then, but avoided the word 'Mama.' We were afraid of how she'd respond."

Pam was naturally comfortable with Emily, because she already had two children of her own. Perhaps because of her dark hair, Emily seemed to be bonding more closely with Pam. So Sherry realized that she had to start doing everything for her child. "Once I made that decision, our bonding was a gradual process. It didn't happen instantly. Slowly, Emily was able to turn toward me when I fed her."

The second week in China, Sherry watched Emily take her first steps in a restaurant, and was lucky enough to capture them on videotape. "She picked up the English language quickly," says Sherry. "She really adjusted, and she is surrounded by people who love her."

One of the ways Sherry and Emily have grown closer is through bubble baths: "Any child of mine would have to love

bubble baths," Sherry explains. "My friends all know that when I answer my phone, 'Poolside!' I'm immersed in bubbles. Emily hated baths at first. She screamed and yelled. Now bubble baths are paradise to her, as they are to me, especially when we are in a tub full of bubbles together."

Emily is two years old now. "She's this little person with a mind that's astounding," Sherry proudly relates. "She's so bright. And she has a big personality. It's larger than life. Very bubbly, very funny. She's got an entertainer's spirit. Totally dramatic. She loves to play jokes on people. She's got a radiant smile with a million dimples. She's also very independent: a strong, decisive, confident person. An old soul. If I wanted to foster something in a child, it would be what she already is."

Emily's last name was originally Huang, after the director who gave every child in her orphanage her own name. "Yang was her first name. It means yellow, the color of the soil of the city she is from. Xin means triple gold, triple prosperous. I kept Yang Xin as Emily's middle name," Sherry says.

She feels it will be hard to tell Emily about her history. "I don't know how to explain that she came from a culture that didn't value women. I can't justify that. The caregivers and the foster families did love those babies dearly, though. I can tell her that."

Recently, Sherry pulled out a box of mementos from China and put them in Emily's room. "Her room is becoming quite a crossroads of the world," she notes. "My family and her godparents bring back dolls from other lands when they travel." But with all the things displayed in her room, Emily was interested in only one thing. She walked up to a picture of a spring scene in China that Sherry had placed on a table.

"China!" Emily exclaimed.

"I got goose bumps all over," says Sherry. "How did she know?"

JIM ROCKWELL

During the fifties and sixties, Jim Rockwell was broadcasting jazz on the radio six nights a week in Detroit. "Later I had a television show on PBS. I always found it impossible to identify with my public persona. I couldn't see myself in pictures. The person I was on the PBS tapes did not resonate with me, though everybody else looked like themselves. I never felt I had a self that I looked like."

Jim, an only child, was adopted by parents who surrounded him with love. "We had little in common but love," he says with a smile. "I didn't look like anyone, and my relatives were all tall. I'm five feet three.

"Looking back, my mom and dad were light years ahead of their time in their openness about my adoption. Bath time was talk time when I was young, and we often talked about it. My mother told me that my birth mother was dying of tuberculosis when I was born. She'd say, 'Your mother was sick and she couldn't be your mother, so I got to be.' She put the good fortune on herself, not on me. I wasn't made to feel grateful. I was always told I was my parents' greatest joy."

Jim lost his parents in an automobile accident in 1954, when he was twenty-nine years old. "I needed to search for my birth family years before I did. My wife, Annie, and I would talk about it. She'd nudge me. I'd say, 'Some day.' But it was age that finally made me begin. I had turned sixty, which seemed old to me at the time. I didn't really know if any of my family was out there, and I wasn't consciously looking for living people because of my age. I had one gnawing thought that kept recurring: 'I have never laid eyes on one living soul whose flesh I am.' It became a need. The older I got, the stronger the need. As

(right) visiting his brother Bill (Carlsbad, California)

Jim graduating from High School, age 17

Amelia Grandchamp, Jim's birth mother

I approached sixty, it became urgent."

The summer he turned sixty-one, Jim and Annie rented a cottage on a lake near Gaylord, Michigan, where he had grown up. With no idea of the laws against searching, they drove to the courthouse in Escanaba, on the Upper Peninsula of Michigan, where Jim knew he had been born. "My folks had told me that my birth mom was French, born in Canada, and that my birth father, who was born in England, had worked for a railroad. There was a young woman behind the counter and I said, 'I'd like to see the birth records for September 13, 1925. I'm looking for a Louis James.' She said, 'We need to have a last name.'" Jim didn't know the last name, but at that moment, he recalled a buried memory, more than five decades old.

"From someplace deep, I remembered a scene when I was very small. I was in the car. It was just Dad and me. I was in the front seat beside him. I don't remember a conversation, I only remember him saying, 'Your family's name was Smith.' I blurted out to the lady behind the counter, 'Try Smith.' She brought out a long narrow file box and began looking at cards. She found September 13, 1925. 'There is no Louis James. There is a Joseph Louis,' she said. 'Let's see if that leads anyplace.'

"The young woman walked into a back room and came out with an enormous journal, the kind in which records were kept ages ago, by hand, with pens dipped in inkwells. There, beside my birth date, was the name Joseph Louis." Jim's mother was indeed French, born in Canada. His father was English, born in London, and he worked for the Soo-Line railroad. "She said, 'This is too much to be coincidence. That's your family.' I said, 'Who are they?'"

"'He was William Henry Smith,' she began. 'She was Amelia Grandchamp [pronounced *Grah-shah*], and they lived in company housing behind the roundhouse in Gladstone.' Now, with this information, she went back to the card file to search again. With every Smith birth she found to those par-

ents, she pulled the card. When she was through, there were cards for six girls and one other boy."

Next, Jim and Annie went to the public library and discovered that in 1927, two years after Jim's birth, his mother's name had disappeared from public records. Assuming that that was when Amelia died, they went the next morning to the City Hall of Gladstone. Jim inquired if there was a lot in the cemetery for the family of William Smith from the 1920s. "The clerk pulled out another of those enormous journals, and said, 'Yes, Amelia is buried there.' Then she said the magic words: 'The care of that lot is paid by Mrs. Kalishek.' Now we had a sister's married name, an unusual name that would be easier to find than a brother with the last name Smith. Annie asked, 'What is Mrs. Kalishek's first name?' The lady said, 'I don't know. They call her Toots.' Annie showed her the list of siblings and asked her who she thought might be Toots. She pointed to Georgina, and said, 'I think that's Toots.'

"She told us that to be certain, we should go to the cemetery," Jim continues. "There would be a stone in the family plot with the name Kalishek." They followed the map and found the stone with Kalishek engraved across the top. On one end, with the dates of birth and death, was the name Clifford. On the other end, with the date of birth but no date of death, was Georgina.

He and Annie drove to a convenience store with a public phone and found Toots' number and address in the directory. "I wanted to call her, but I was too scared. We found her address and drove by, just to look. She lives in an apartment building for elderly folks. We drove to the address where the family lived when I was born. We stopped and sat for a while, just looking at the house. Then we returned to the convenience store.

"I asked Annie, 'What do I say to this lady? How do I explain this call?' Annie said, 'Don't try to explain on the phone. Just ask if we can come and see her, and when you're face to face, you can tell her who you are.'"

Jim placed the call. "A woman answered," he remembers. "I said, 'I'm looking for the family of William and Amelia Smith.' She said, 'Well, I'm one.' I said, 'May I come see you? I think we're related.' She asked, 'Is this little brother Jimmy?' I said, 'I think so.' She asked for my birthday and when I told her, she said, 'Oh, my God, Jimmy!'"

While Jim and Annie drove to her apartment, Toots, who was seventy-one, called another sister, seventy-four-year-old Vinie. "Come over here right now. Our brother Jimmy is on his way!" Then she went down to the lobby and waited for him by the big glass doors. "As we walked up the sidewalk she came toward me. I can still feel the physical, gut reaction I had when I saw her face and recognized my own.

"Upstairs in her apartment, the first thing Toots said was, 'You were the fourteenth child.' I was always included in the family count: fourteen children, not thirteen. When she showed us family pictures, I saw the 'look' we all shared. I saw the faces. I saw a photo of my mother, Amelia. Toots opened a cubbyhole drawer in her desk and took out an envelope. She said, 'I knew someday I would give you this.' Inside the envelope marked 'All Saints Church' was my baptismal certificate. She had saved it for sixty-one years. She could put her hands on it in an instant.

"She told me that four of my brothers were artists, cartoon animators in motion pictures. I grew up seeing their work: Woody Woodpecker, Tom and Jerry, Mr. Magoo, Gulliver's Travels, Popeye, Peanuts. A world of animated characters. My oldest brother, Paul, at eighteen, hopped a freight train out of Gladstone and rode all the way to Hollywood. He became Walt Disney's eighteenth employee, before Disney was well known, before Mickey Mouse. The next brother, Frank, followed when he turned eighteen, hopping freight trains across the country to Hollywood. Finally, Bill, my only brother still living, got there by freight train and Model T Ford. The three brothers sent a passenger train ticket to my brother Hank when he turned eighteen. Hank joined them as a cartoonist at the studio. Bill left animation in the 1940s and became a sculptor. The rest had long careers in the studios. There is now a second generation of Smiths in the film industry. Paul's daughter Sheryl is in animation, doing delightful art, including *The Little Mermaid*. Frank's son Charlie is Charles Martin Smith, an actor and director, who had on-screen roles in *American Graffiti* and *Never Cry Wolf*.

When Vinie arrived, I saw her reaction when she looked at my face. 'That's Jimmy!' Soon the apartment was filled with relatives. They agreed that we would all get together that afternoon at the home of one of Toots' daughters." Within hours of Jim's arrival, sixty-seven people knew about it.

That day, Jim discovered that after being separated from the family because of his mother's illness, he had been taken to an orphanage on Lake Superior. Later, the orphanage sent the family a picture of Jim at about six months old. They had the picture enlarged and put in a big oval frame. Over the years it hung in the home of one family member or another. For many years it was in an upstairs bedroom in Vinie's house. "In the back yard with all those people, one of Vinie's daughters came up to me and said, 'I've been looking at a baby picture of you all of my life!' I asked, 'Have I changed?' She said, 'You've got the same amount of hair.'"

During the course of the afternoon, Jim learned more about his family. "My birth father was 55 when I was born. My mother was 45. In my father's later years, he would always say, 'I have to live long enough to find Jimmy.' Amelia was a tiny lady, 4'10", thin, and frail. Yet she baked six loaves of bread every day. She did laundry constantly and earned tuition for her children's Catholic education by doing more laundry for the nuns. Through it all, it seems she was a very funny lady. There is a vein of humor that runs through us all, the same kind of humor. At one point in the afternoon, my nephew Bud sidled over, introduced himself, and just stood there. Finally, he leaned toward me and queried, 'Has anyone asked you for money yet?' 'No, you're the first,' I replied.

"We found a lot more than six sisters and a brother that day. We found fifty nieces and nephews and their children and their children's children. I grew up an only child, as did Annie, and we didn't have children, so I was never around them. I didn't know how to talk to them or play with them. Now, little ones would run and throw themselves on me to hug and play, and it was an epiphany: the joy of a child's hug. This child, running to hug me, is part of me. We're connected by generations.

"The genetic markers are so strong. My brother and I speak the same way. The way we play with words, the way we phrase our thoughts. When we're together, we often don't finish our sentences. I grew up in a very different environment, very different influences and cultural input, yet I've never been so as one with anyone. We are alike.

"That first day in Toots' apartment, she asked if I had pictures of myself as a boy. I said I would send her some. Two days later we were back in the Lower Peninsula with a cousin from my adoptive family, telling him about finding my family. I told him about my sister wanting pictures and he said, 'I have lots of pictures of you as a kid. She can have some of these.' The first one he put on the table was my high school senior photo. Just two days before, I had seen the family look. Now I saw it again, in my face. That picture jumped off the table at me and said, 'Look, Jim, this is who you were all that time.'

"After meeting my birth family, I felt what is known as 'mirror hunger.' I'd get up in the middle of the night to look in the mirror and see the family resemblance in me. And then, gradually, I began to see the me in me.

"At the end of the summer, when it was time to go back to Texas, I couldn't leave the place where I grew up without going to the cemetery where my adoptive parents are buried. I hadn't done that in more than twenty years. I was compelled to go there, to stand at my mom's grave and to say out loud, 'You're still my mother.'"

Jim lost Annie in 1990. He lives now in the Upper Peninsula of Michigan, not far from Gladstone, in a little cottage in the woods beside the Escanaba River.

"To know who I am, the self discovery, was at the heart of my searching. Who am I really? Now I know. The identity that for so long felt acquired, now feels real and whole. While visiting a nephew one day, he stopped in mid-sentence and said, 'Look at how you're sitting. That's my dad.' His father had been gone for years. I ache that I didn't know him, that I didn't know all of my brothers and sisters. Yet I thrill that I'm embraced by this loving family, who tell me so much about myself, even when not saying a word."

"IN OUR SMALL RURAL TOWN OF PALMYRA, MISSOURI, THE ONLY PLACE TO get condoms two for a quarter was in the men's bathroom at the Texaco station. I'd go with my girlfriend. One of us stood guard while the other rushed in with all our quarters, and got as many condoms as she could. At the time, it seemed like a bargain—until January 13, 1968, when my twelve-and-a-half-cent condom broke.

"We were in my boyfriend's old car, in the back seat, at a local farm where everyone parked, and it was winter. I had on knee socks, held up with rubber bands. I was so young—sixteen is so young. I knew that night that I was pregnant.

"Now, in Missouri, if you got pregnant, you had to quit high school. The boy had to quit, too, and neither could come back until a year after the baby was born." Delores' parents had divorced three years earlier, and her mother had moved to Oregon. When Delores realized she was pregnant, she quit school, told everyone she missed her mother, and flew to Oregon, where pregnant girls were permitted to attend night school. "I threw up on the plane," she recalls. "My mother greeted me and said, 'You don't look right. Is something wrong with you?' She took me to the doctor to be checked for the flu and sure enough, I was pregnant."

Delores' mother and stepfather wanted her to marry her boyfriend, but his parents said that was out of the question. Then her parents urged her to file a paternity suit. Delores was furious. "You are not going to make me get married!" she told them. "I'm going to college and I'm going to be somebody." Her parents were speechless.

...res on the bridge leading to the Maternity Home in Oregon

Six months before her due date, Delores entered a Salvation Army maternity home about one hundred miles from her mother's house. The Salvation Army is an international religious and charitable organization, but it is organized and operated with a military hierarchy: Officers are ranked from Lieutenant to Brigadier, and all wear uniforms. Some girls in the home had parents who paid for their stay. These girls lived on the second floor. "They had beautiful birds'-eye maple furniture, drapes, shutters, woven rugs, and a big claw-foot tub down the hall. And they had velour towels," Delores remembers. "But my dad was not sending any money, so I was on the third floor, with the other girls who couldn't afford to pay. We lived in a large dorm room with old metal showers and plain cotton army surplus towels."

Soon Delores persuaded an elderly sergeant to let her have one of the two closet-sized private rooms with a tiny gabled window and a small sink. "I had this little world of my own. I tore out fashion models' photos and put them all over the walls. And I always tried to get Bernice, the sergeant, to give me a velour towel like the girls on the second floor had.

"We went to church twice a week. We were told to pray for forgiveness—we were sinners. And penance for our sin was giving up our babies. That was how we would make peace with God. The sergeants told us no boys would marry us if we admitted to having a baby. They said we were wise to keep this secret between ourselves and God.

"There wasn't much to do," Delores remembers. "I read every book in the lending library. You could make crafts and ceramics. You could play pool and watch TV. Someone donated a beauty parlor shampoo bowl so we could shampoo each other's hair. To get to the bus for downtown Portland, we crossed a moss-covered concrete bridge. Sometimes we walked down the hill to Montgomery Ward. Seven or eight of us would waddle down, wearing fake wedding bands, our bodies colliding like bumper cars. If anyone asked, we were told to say our husbands were in Vietnam.

"Sewing was forbidden on Sundays. Since I never had any visitors, I nearly went out of my mind on Sundays. The sewing room was an old porch at the end of the second floor, past the quarters where the sergeants and lieutenants in residence lived. If you could sneak down there, you could shut the door, take the machine on the end, and no one could hear you. On Sundays I would tiptoe down, gently shut the door, and sew all day. I was sewing dresses for when my life would begin again.

"We lived for our Thursday visits from the young resident physician, who was terribly handsome. It was like a date for all fifty-seven of us, ages thirteen to twenty-eight. The night before, we'd set our hair in giant pink rollers. We put on lipstick while listening to "Born to be Wild" on the record player. Before seeing the doctor, the nurses had us take off our underwear so we'd be ready when he called us in. So there we were, waiting in line, fifty-seven sexually frustrated, formerly sexually active, young women with all our makeup on, holding our panties wrapped in a brown paper towel.

"The doctor induced as many of us as he could each Thursday. If you were in the ballpark of your due date, he gave you a pink slip. That was your ticket out. We were induced with buccal pitocin, which is now outlawed because it caused erratic and extremely intense labor."

Delores was induced prematurely at nine-thirty, and her water broke at one o'clock. "I wasn't allowed any visitors, no phone calls, no contact by parents or relatives. I was put in leather restraints to keep me from thrashing. My hands were tied to the bed rails. At the end, they gave me a spinal, so I wouldn't feel the pushing. I labored alone. It was hell. I wanted human contact, someone to talk to." At six-fifty p.m., Delores gave birth to a son. "They placed a large screen across my belly, so I couldn't see or touch my baby. The doctor did tell me that it was a boy. He said, 'He looks like a basketball player.'

"Three of us delivered that day. They gave us each a shot to dry up our milk and a green antiseptic 'soup' to squirt in our vaginas. From our rooms, we could hear our babies crying, but we were not permitted to see them. We were told, 'You promised your baby for adoption. A nice family is waiting.' During our required ten-day stay in the hospital, our babies were there for the first five. Five days of hearing their cries was torture."

Delores confronted the nurses to no avail. They stood behind policy, and wouldn't bend an inch. She was enraged. At one point, she shouted, "You either bring him to me now, or I will walk out with him!" Delores had no idea how she'd accomplish this, but it didn't matter. A caseworker was summoned, and a deal was cut. "Looking back, I say I made a deal with the devil. The nurses agreed to sneak me into the 'Mothers' Room.' But I wasn't allowed to tell the others, and I had to swear to sign all the papers on the fifth day.

"For five days, I rocked my baby, crying. I remember Donovan's song "Lalania" was on the radio. I wanted to bring my son home, though there was no way I could. But I also

school room, the business office, the waiting room. As we walked, people stepped out to ask about my son. For the full length of the hallway, I was his mother.

"When I reached the end, I handed my baby to the caseworker. I promised him, 'I'll come get you,' and then I cried all the way back down the hall. This time, I returned to the 'No Mothers' room. When we turned off the lights for bed, every woman in the room began to cry. Huge grief, huge grief," she recalls sadly.

In January, amidst rumors and speculation about her absence, Delores returned to Missouri to finish high school. On her first day back, the principal called her to his office. He said he believed her night school transcripts were faked, that she'd actually moved to Oregon to have a baby. "But I earned those grades, and I told him I was there to get an education. He didn't want to admit me until I confessed about the baby.

"WHEN I REACHED THE END, I HANDED MY BABY TO THE CASEWORKER. I PROMISED HIM, 'I'LL COME GET YOU,' AND THEN I CRIED ALL THE WAY BACK DOWN THE HALL. THIS TIME, I RETURNED TO THE 'NO MOTHERS' ROOM.'"

---

wanted to finish my education, and I was told that he would be raised by a loving family who would provide him with the best of everything. So the choice made sense."

On October 8 at 9:30 a.m., the caseworker knocked on the door to the Mothers' Room, and asked Delores to sign two papers. By signing the first, she surrendered her baby for adoption. "I didn't realize it at the time, because it was not explained to me, but when I signed the second paper, I gave up my right to change my mind within six months.

"At 11:30, my son was brought to me. I changed his clothes and put him in little kitty-cat pajamas the foster home had sent over. All the while, I talked to him. I told him I would come get him. I told him I was sorry. I sobbed.

"A nurse knocked on the door. 'It's time now,' she said. I asked, 'Why don't you let me walk him down the hall?' All along the hallway were different rooms: the kitchen, the

We sat in his office for an hour as he stonewalled me. He peeled an orange and became madder and madder. I wasn't going to tell him if it was the last thing I did.

"Finally, he slammed his fist on the desk and said, 'Fine, you can go to school here, but you are not to be on the honor roll, you are not to be on the cheerleaders' squad, you are not to associate with the other kids. I expect you to be isolated from everyone else.' I made sure I looked really good every day, had great clothes, studied really hard, made great grades, and graduated. A few kids slowly came around and became friends, but most felt I had been a bad girl."

When she was just out of high school, a scout for the Ford Modeling Agency asked Delores to come to New York. Delores chose nursing school instead. During the next seventeen years, she worked in terminal care oncology, and cared for indigent, pregnant women living on the street. Delores was

taught music. Both were tall, upper-class, and in their late thirties. Delores called every university in Oregon, looking for professors of philosophy who matched the description. After exhausting her own attempts, she used the state-assisted search program, which opens the sealed file and uses an intermediary to make contact with the child.

"My son told them he wanted to meet me, so they sent him paperwork to fill out. I waited and waited." Her son's paperwork was never returned. Delores worried that the impersonal nature of the state system had intimidated him. She wanted to mail a letter to him, to make herself 'real.' After checking Oregon law, she found nothing that indicated it was illegal to send a letter with non-identifying information. Yet the agency refused.

Delores' personal frustration led her to become an activist. She contacted the governor's office and the attorney general's office. People at the State Department were beginning to know the tenacious Mrs. Teller.

One night Delores, who was desperate by now, attended a farewell dinner for a woman who had worked at the agency that placed her son. Amidst the balloons, Delores asked if they could speak alone, and tried to convince the woman to send the letter she had written to her son. "Since she would no longer be working at the agency, I figured she had nothing to lose. After she refused, I asked her to think about it and placed the letter on her desk. Two weeks later, the letter came back to me. I was devastated."

Now running out of options, Delores resorted to more extreme measures. "I had been given the name of someone who had been known to help people in my situation. I called and left a message. That night I woke up at two in the morning in tremendous grief. I was in a black hole. I sobbed to my husband, 'I guess I've done terrible things in my life. Why can't I find my son? Why won't they let me have his name?' My husband held me and I cried and cried. Finally, I fell asleep. I was in the final day of saying an eight-day novena to

shopping in a department store when a woman asked if she would consider modeling a couture line for I. Magnin and Nordstrom. She agreed, and many of the younger models began asking her for advice on hair, makeup, and photos. Slowly, Delores started booking her own models and putting on shows for I. Magnin. Eventually, she started her own business.

Today, Delores has been married for more than twenty years. She reared two sons and one daughter. But all her adult life, she has lived with the memory of the son she had in the Salvation Army home. On the day he turned eighteen, she began to search for him. "Intuitively, I felt he needed me," she says.

A social worker told her that the adoptive father was a professor of philosophy at a local university, and that his wife

St. Jude, the patron saint of hopeless cases.

"The following morning, that person returned my call. Within a few hours, we were sitting in a coffee shop, sharing our stories. There was a man behind me, playing "Misty" on his guitar. My mother is an entertainer, and "Misty" is her theme song; I feel it has come to me at significant times in my life.

"My companion leaned across the table and asked, 'Do you know what the penalty is in Oregon for divulging information in adoption records?' As I began to reply, this person said, 'I don't think you understand me. They put people in jail for this.' All the while, my mother's song was playing. I said that I understood the consequences, but I had to find my son. 'His name is Marshall Whitaker,' my companion said finally. 'He lives in Pittsburgh, Pennsylvania. There are those who believe a mother has a right to know her children.' I sat there in shock. It was the eighth day of my novena."

Delores spent three frustrating days tracking down his telephone number. Finally, she found the right one.

"I called and called, first at decent hours, then pretty soon at three in the morning. Finally, on a Tuesday night I reached his landlord, who was feeding Marshall's cat. It turned out that Marshall had been away on business. I hesitated at first, but then I left my name. I was sure he would call, and he did. The first thing Marshall said was, 'I knew you were coming. I just didn't know when you would get here.' The next day he FedEx-ed photographs of himself, and enclosed a note that read, 'I've waited twenty-eight years to hear your voice again.'

"I learned that Marshall had been adopted by two college students from the coast of Oregon. The father was not a philosophy professor. The mother was not a music teacher. They were short, not tall like me. They qualified because one of their grandmothers had a lot of money. But when Marshall was five years old, his parents divorced, and he lived with his mother. When he was seven, she left him with his father. His mother came to get him after a year, and they moved from place to place. She remarried, and they moved to Pittsburgh. Her new husband and Marshall did not get along. True to the doctor's prediction, Marshall was a wonderful basketball player, but his parents kicked him out of the house and he was on his own from the age of sixteen. He didn't finish high school, and went into the navy at eighteen.

"It was a real shock to me to find out his life had been far more difficult than I ever imagined. But there was a point where I had to accept that I could do nothing about any of it. I did the best I could."

ALL OF HIS LIFE, BARRIE SHIBLEY WALKED TWO PATHS. BUT UNTIL HE AND his wife began the process of adopting their first daughter, Samantha, he was only aware of one. He did not know that his original path began with a dark legacy.

"Although I always knew, growing up, that I was adopted, whenever I asked my parents where I came from, I saw a look of discomfort on their faces. They brushed the whole thing aside." Barrie decided that if the topic made them so uncomfortable, he would not pursue it. He had a close relationship with his adoptive parents, and felt that his questions were not that important.

Barrie's adoptive parents had been told by Social Services that his birth mother, unable to care for him, had brought him to their office to be placed for adoption. "When the social worker handed my parents this little brown baby, she said, 'Look at his coloring. He has a dark complexion and so do you folks. It's going to be a nice match. Just make him one of yours. Don't tell him he's Indian.'"

In the seventies, when he was a teenager, Barrie's parents finally told him he had been born in Lestock, Saskatchewan. "When I looked on a map, I saw it was near an Indian reserve. And there was no doubt, when I stared into the mirror, that I looked Indian. When I asked my parents, they admitted I was part Indian, but told me not to worry: 'There is other stuff in there, too, so you'll be okay,' they said. Still, I never wanted to search. It didn't matter to me."

His attitude changed after he married Val, an attorney who runs a general law practice.

Barrie standing amidst the
Hoodoos in Banff, Alberta

39

Barrie is president of a public company involved in natural gas and other types of energy production. They live in Alberta, Canada. Though Barrie remained reluctant, Val had always wanted to know more about her husband's heritage; she had grown up around Indian people, and never considered his heritage to be a stigma. She knew wealthy Indian families, some who ran their own logging businesses. "To me, not knowing everything you can possibly know about yourself is incomprehensible," Val says. "Our infertility was the perfect excuse for me to get more information about Barrie's background."

In 1989, after sending a request for non-identifying information to the Department of Indian Affairs, Barrie received a call informing him that he was a treaty status Indian. This means that he is a registered Indian, affiliated with a band that signed a treaty. "The caller told me I was with the Carry The Kettle First Nation. My given name was Vernon Rope. At one time, my birth family's name was Medicine Rope, but they shortened it to Rope. My birth mother was Sally Rope. I am an Assiniboin Sioux. We were Plains Indians. In the late 1800's, the Sioux were in the Dakotas with Sitting Bull when General Custer attacked at Little Big Horn. Our tribe fled to Saskatchewan. I was stunned by this news. I was amazed that I was a part of this fantastic history."

The first birth family member Barrie found was his older half-brother Colin, a social worker, who lived nearby. "I phoned him at his office and asked, 'Is this Colin Rope, and are you from the Carry The Kettle reserve?' He said, 'Yeah.' I quizzed him about what I had learned, and after he answered all my questions correctly, I told him I believed we were brothers. There was dead silence on the line. Finally he said, 'You're kidding.' I said, 'My name is Barrie Shibley, but my birth name was Vernon.' Now I could tell he was really stunned. At last he said, 'My cousin Juanita and I were talking about you just last night. We were remembering when the government came to take you away, and wondering if you would ever find us. Get down here right now!'"

Barrie jumped into his car and drove straight to Colin's office. "Colin stood up and came toward me," Barrie recalls. "A big, gregarious guy. We shook hands. When he called Juanita to tell her, she went wild. I could hear her screaming and wailing through the phone."

Barrie learned from Colin that his three older siblings had been placed in residential schools run by churches, and that they could only return home during some summers. It was a social policy of the Canadian government to go in and 'scoop' up children from the reserve, placing them in residential schools or foster care. "Some were adopted into white families, in an attempt to assimilate them and rob them of their culture," Barrie says. "The intention was to make them 'valuable members of society.' In many such schools, Indian children were beaten for speaking their native language or for practicing their culture in any way. No government services were provided for Indian families with problems, and no attempt was made to rehabilitate them.

"It is a horrible legacy," Barrie reflects. "My birth mother was poor and never had a man she could count on. She didn't abuse her children. She wasn't an alcoholic. She was a native woman living all by herself. Social Services came in and apprehended her children. She didn't voluntarily surrender them. Years after they took my three older siblings, the government came for me. I was four months old."

A few days after they first met, Barrie and Colin drove together to Saskatchewan so Barrie could meet their mother, Sally. They registered at a nearby motel, and Barrie stayed behind while Colin went to Sally's to prepare her for his visit. Barrie remembers, "When I finally walked through the door, she grabbed me and would not let me go. She was so shaken. She didn't want me to leave again.

"She told me she had looked for us for a long time," he recalls. "She wandered through schoolyards looking for her children. For years, she would take buses and visit different schools. Of course, she never found us. Then she told me that there were two younger children who had also been taken. After I was seized, Sally tried to hide these children at another reserve. But Social Services caught up with her and seized them, too. That's when she had a nervous breakdown. She couldn't remember their names because she was mugged and beaten on her way to the community hall to play bingo one night. The beating caused a minor brain injury. She asked me to find the last two, so all her children would be with her. She said that she had been waiting for me to come back so I could find them."

Sally's two youngest children are full siblings to Barrie. "My birth father is out there somewhere. I have no need for him. When I think of the position he put Sally in, it makes my blood run cold. If the phone rang tomorrow and he said he'd like to meet me for coffee, I'd give him fifteen minutes. But it would have to be a hell of a good fifteen minutes for him to get any more time. Sally didn't say much about him. She was very quiet, very gentle, typically native. The Indian tendency is not to talk, but to listen. Listen, and say few words."

Barrie and Colin immediately planned to locate their younger siblings. Colin remembered hearing about a guy with the last name Rope who worked in concrete construction. When they found him, he was living three blocks from Sally and never knew it. His life had been very difficult. He had been through many foster homes and was never adopted. By the time he entered his last foster home, he was a teenager, and those foster parents became his Mom and Dad. His new father was a solid influence, and his death a few years later was a devastating loss.

"My younger brother and his wife came to meet us," Barrie recalls. "The day before we were supposed to meet, he parked outside our house in his truck, and watched me from a distance to make sure I was okay. The next day, as we got to know each other, Val stared at my brother, and his wife stared at me. We looked so much alike."

It took Barrie and Colin quite a while to locate their last

Emily (foreground), Samantha, and Jennifer posing in front of their home in Calgary, Alberta

missing sibling, a little sister. "About a year later, I received a phone call that I almost didn't return. But my secretary insisted that it sounded really important. The caller said her last name was Rope and she thought she was my sister. I was thrilled and shocked that she had been able to find me.

"With her typical quirky humor, she asked, 'Where the hell have you been?' After being taken from Sally, she'd been placed in more than twenty foster homes. By age five, she still wasn't talking. Social Services thought she had developmental problems. But a loving family adopted her when she was six,

41

and she blossomed. She graduated from college, and now counsels native women. Colin took her to meet Sally right away."

Barrie's younger brother on the other hand, had declined to meet Sally, though he had driven by her home and watched her from a distance. When Sally suddenly became critically ill and was rushed to the hospital with little hope of living much longer, Barrie hated the thought that she would never meet her youngest son. "When I heard Sally was in the hospital, I dropped everything and drove eight hours to see her that night," he recalls.

"The doctors asked us to make decisions about quality of care and whether to resuscitate. Colin said she would not want to be hooked up to machines. I called my younger brother from the hospital and told him he might be making a mistake he'd regret for the rest of his life. I said, 'You don't have time to think about it. Just come now.' He visited her the next day. As it turned out, Sally lived six months longer, but died knowing her children were all alive and safe."

Barrie can't imagine what his life would have been like if he'd grown up on the reserve. His adoptive family is very close, and he sees his parents and his sister all the time. However, finding his birth family changed his life, and Val's. "Because Barrie is native, we naturally wanted to adopt native children," Val explains. "Samantha, who is ten, is a Cree. Jennifer, six, is a Blood Indian. By marrying Barrie, I have treaty status even though I am not native. So does our three-year-old Emily, who was born to us.

"When Jennifer was three," recalls Val, "we rented the movie 'The Indian in the Cupboard'. The main character puts up his tent in a child's room, sets a fire, and dances around the flames. Jennifer's birth mother is a wonderful native dancer. The next day, Jennifer was up in her room for hours. When I went to check on her, I saw she had made a fire out of colored paper and surrounded it with bits of brown paper to represent stones. She was doing a pow-wow dance around the fire. She wasn't pretending to be the little Indian in the movie—she is Indian."

"Before 1989, I was in limbo," Barrie reflects. "That year, I gained a past, my heritage, and a future, my children, all in one stroke. Finding my history enables me to walk two paths in two different worlds. I want my daughters to grow up knowing and being Indians. As adults they will carry in their hearts the sadness of what happened to their people. They will know their personal heritage, the true story of their birth families, and as they want more information, we will give it to them. I want them to be proud of their heritage. They will be able to walk in two worlds."

IN THE FINAL MONTHS OF HER PREGNANCY, THE BIRTH MOTHER OF KELSEY Kangas changed her mind. She had been working with an adoption agency that facilitated closed adoptions. But she realized she couldn't allow the social worker at the agency—whom she barely knew—to choose the parents who would raise her child. With a decision of this magnitude, she couldn't trust anyone but herself. She decided that she needed to meet the people who would love and care for her child. So she found a new adoption agency that assisted in open adoptions.

One month before Kelsey was born, her adoptive parents and her birth parents met for the first time. "That first evening, the four of them placed their hands on my birth mother's belly and felt me moving around," says Kelsey, now sixteen.

Kelsey was three-and-a-half years old when her birth parents married. On their honeymoon, they bought her a wicker rocking horse, meant for Kelsey to use and then pass on to her children. "When I was little, I played on that rocking horse all the time," Kelsey says.

"My parents have always said, 'You've known your whole life that you've been adopted.' I have always been told I was very special. But most people don't realize I'm adopted. My adoptive mom is real tan and my adoptive dad is tall, six foot six, with curly hair. I remember one of my teachers saying, 'I see you get your complexion from your mom and your height and your hair from your dad.' And I said, 'Yeah.' I didn't want to explain it."

When Kelsey was eight, her classmates were teasing each other during recess about being 'accidents.' "We were all saying to each other, 'No one wanted you here,'" she recalls. "Back in class I began thinking, 'Wow! I actually was an accident!' The thought had never crossed my mind before. Then I wondered about why my birth parents gave me up—wasn't I good enough? A split second later my mom's voice came into my head saying, 'They loved you so much that they trusted us to raise you.' It was perplexing to me, though.

"I remember standing in our kitchen when I was about five years old, listening to my mom talk on the telephone," Kelsey says. "I was so young, but I remember thinking, 'Wow, she's talking to my birth mother!' My mom asked if I wanted to talk to her. I was too scared. Maybe I was too embarrassed, or felt she might not like me."

Kelsey met her birth parents for the first time when she was eleven. "That was a really big day," she recalls. "It was a Saturday, and I had gone out. When I came home, my mom and birth mother were on the deck talking. My mom always says she would have been friends with my birth mother if they had met in college. They clicked right away."

Kelsey didn't know what to expect when her adoptive mother brought her out to the deck to meet her birth mother. "I was shaky, and kind of sick to my stomach, I was so nervous," she recalls. "We said hi, and hugged, and we both got teary-eyed."

After they all talked for a while, Kelsey's adoptive parents went for a walk. "My birth mother and I had an hour and a half, just the two of us talking," she says. 'There's a special bond between us because she is my mother by blood. She picked two great people for me to live with. I am so happy that she is not ashamed of me, like some people who never want to have anything to do with the children they put up for adoption. I don't know how I would deal with it if she were ashamed of me."

Kelsey loves to speculate about what her life would have been like if her birth parents had chosen a different family. "I used to ask my mom, 'What if I had a twin? Would you have kept my twin, or would you have kept me?' My mom would

say, 'Oh honey, I would have loved you both.' Before I had the courage to ask her if I might have a twin, I did think it was kind of a neat idea. But actually I'm glad there's not some other me floating around out there that I don't know about."

Just before meeting her birth parents, Kelsey learned they had other children. "My mom got off the phone with them and said, 'Okay. Now, the oldest boy is six, the daughter is three, and the youngest son is eight months old.' I thought, 'Wow! I have two brothers and a sister.' But they're not really my brothers and sister. I'm still not spending time with them, and they don't know who I am to them. So the connection's just by blood. At first I was so excited about having a younger sister. I've never had a younger sibling. I thought, 'Wouldn't it be neat if, when my sister gets older, we could be close and have a relationship. She could stay with me. I'd show her around and we'd go shopping.'"

A few years later, Kelsey finally met her three full siblings at one of her brother's hockey games. "I was introduced as a 'special friend' of my birth mother. I just wanted to cry. They didn't realize who I was. So I was just like, 'Oh, hi. I'm Kelsey, and how are you?' Meeting them was really a big thing for me. There is a picture of me on their mantel. I can't wait until they're older and they can know. Actually, my birth mother thinks my oldest brother might know already. I really don't know how they will react. They may feel I am not at all a part of their family. Or they might completely accept me. They may even be angry that I'm not part of their family, or that they were never told about me. I know I could never be mad at my mom if she told me she gave up a child for adoption. I would understand, because I know what that's like. But at least my brothers and sister have met me. And someday when they're older, we will have a mature conversation about it.

"I have a fantasy that when I get my driver's license, I will drive to my birth family's house and take my sister and brothers out for ice cream. If my adoptive mother feels that's too far to drive, she can come with me!"

Kelsey floating (Cadillac, Michigan)

A family picnic in Madrona Canyon (Larkspur, California)

THE VIDEO TAKEN IN HER CRIB AT THE ROMANIAN ORPHANAGE SHOWED EIGHT-month-old Katerina wet with urine from the chest down. The only diapers available in the orphanage were leaky and gauze-like. Her crib sheet was drenched. As they viewed the video at the offices of the Adopt International Agency, Sherwood and Jan Cummins were already totally in love with the little girl; they had spent the entire weekend looking at photographs of her.

On the previous Friday, Sherwood had attended an orientation at the agency's offices. Photographs of nineteen available children were passed around. Sherwood was the last to see them. "When I got halfway through the pictures, I saw her and said to myself, 'Oh, my God! That's my daughter!' I knew if I were the first one in line, nobody else would have seen that picture. I would have taken it and tucked it up my sleeve. I was in love. My heart connected with this little girl. The picture looked just like Jan's baby pictures. I saw the look of awe in this child, and how bright her eyes were. I couldn't imagine that this picture had gone through twenty hands and she was still available. The next day, when Jan returned from her business trip, I took her suitcases and sat her down on the couch. The photographs of Katerina were displayed in front of her. Just like me, Jan fell completely in love."

Sherwood and Jan live in Marin County, California, just north of the Golden Gate Bridge. They never considered domestic adoption, because they felt a teenage birth mother would most likely think of them as grandparents (Sherwood was sixty; Jan was

47

Katerina playing mother to baby sister Gabriella

forty-four). It was unlikely they could find an agency that would approve them for the same reason. Also, neither felt they could endure a birth mother changing her mind, as sometimes happens in domestic adoptions.

They learned about Romanian orphans from a segment aired on the television show *20/20*, as well as from numerous newspaper and magazine articles. News of the plight of these children had captured national attention. "The children looked like caged animals on the television shows," Jan recalls. "It was just awful."

Under Romanian dictator Ceausescu's regime, women were not permitted to use birth control. Every family was ordered to produce five children, regardless of whether or not they could afford them. Most could not. Ceausescu's plan was to increase the country's military force. "The government literally warehoused the children in these orphanages, because their families could not afford to care for them. Parents were desperate," Sherwood explains. "At one point, when Ceausescu learned the children were becoming weak, he had them transfused to make them stronger. They would use the same needle for many children. That fresh pint of blood was often HIV-positive."

By the time Sherwood and Jan decided to adopt, the regime had already ended with the assassination of Ceausescu and his wife. In its aftermath, 13,000 children

under the age of three were available for adoption. "The agency provided encouraging information that gave us hope of getting a healthy child," Jan says. "With that, we went forward with plans to adopt, our hearts wide open, ignoring the often dire predictions from news stories about the health of the children at these orphanages."

After the regime, the employment rate in Romania was only eighteen percent. "We learned through Katerina's special caregiver in the orphanage, Lavinia, who was employed by the adoption agency, that Katerina's father was a bricklayer," Sherwood says. "He was working right up to the end of the regime. After the revolution began, his money was valueless. His job ended. Before the revolution, he was in the process of building a two-story home for the family. All the walls were done, but there was no floor and now he had no money to put a floor in. The top story wasn't finished. There was no heat. After the regime ended, he and his wife were only financially able to keep six of their children. The seventh and eighth children were taken by an uncle. Katerina was the ninth. Her parents were working for other families in exchange for food and clothing. They were not lazy. They wanted to work for what they got. But there was no money to be had."

After flying to Romania, Sherwood and Jan drove to the Corabia orphanage to pick up Katerina. "In the beautiful countryside, we'd see twenty men standing around in a field, willing to work, but there would be only two shovels," Jan remembers. "Gypsies traveled the roads in their wagons. Elderly women with pitch forks worked in the fields. There was no machinery. Everything was done by hand."

The entrance to the orphanage was dark. On a table near the door, Sherwood and Jan left gifts—soaps, lotions, and T-shirts, for the caregivers and other personnel, including the drivers. Then they went straight into the crib room.

"We were pretty shocked when we walked in. The room was very, very small and incredibly hot. The bathroom was dark, with cement slab walls. That's where they were all bathed, and the kids were scared to death of baths; it must have been a horrible experience for them," Jan says. "Our perception from the media coverage was that the children were not cared for. We found that the caregivers at the orphanage were very loving. There just weren't enough people to go around."

Sherwood recalls, "One of the nurses was holding Katerina. Four children were left in her crib room. Two others had been adopted in the last two weeks. The remaining four had twice witnessed two unfamiliar people enter their room, pick up a child, and they never saw their crib mate again. So when they put Katerina in Jan's arms, she began to scream."

"There was no time for a transition. She was just handed over," Jan recalls. "I froze. The nurse took her back and they brought her into the playroom. Katerina didn't seem very comfortable, as if she hadn't been in there often. She was supposed to have been out of her crib for two hours each day, but I'm not sure it was that much. The children did everything in their cribs, because there was no one available to supervise them when they were out of the cribs."

"One child was rocking back and forth, and banging his head for self-stimulation," Sherwood recalls. "Children like that would probably not be adoptable. They were considered too damaged to ever recover. And yet he was a very beautiful child."

That night in the hotel room, Sherwood made his first true connection with Katerina, when she threw her pink horse toy. "I picked it up and tossed it back onto her lap. She picked it up and threw it on mine. This little game was our first interaction. Jan and I had learned a few Romanian terms of endearment, but we primarily communicated with body language, tone of voice, and touch."

In the Corabia orphanage, the children's food was pureed and diluted with water, so they could bottle-feed themselves. They were never given solid food, because that would have required more attention than the caregivers could provide. "When we brought Katerina home, I fed her from a bottle. That was kind of nice, because it gave me the experience of

having a 'baby,' even though she was already fifteen months old. She actually did not eat solid food for a long time," Jan says. "The first few days she was nervous about venturing out of her room. It might be that if she had crawled out of her crib room at the orphanage, she would have been disciplined. With so many children, they needed to keep order."

At first, Jan worried about whether Katerina could become close to her. "One time Katerina fell at the playground and ran to someone else for comfort, which was devastating." she recalls. Jan sought support from other adoptive mothers to boost her confidence. As adopted children learn to identify their mother, she was told, it's important that they are not consoled by anyone else. At the very least, she would need to be involved in the process.

"A year later, when Katerina was two-and-a-half, she began saying, 'Mommy, Daddy, me want baby sister,'" Sherwood remembers. "We asked ourselves if she really knew that she had a sister. My intuition said to follow up on the idea."

"The day we found out there was a sister was Columbus Day, so I was home from work," Jan remembers. "The agency called. As it turned out, five months after Katerina left the orphanage, her birth mother had another daughter. Katerina had no way of knowing she had a baby sister. But somehow she just knew."

Against the advice of friends and the agency, Sherwood and Jan took Katerina to the orphanage to get her sister. They

felt she was too much a part of it all to be left at home. Katerina had very high expectations. For eight months she told everybody they were going to go get her baby sister. She promised Jan she would share her baby sister with her. "Katerina knew from pictures that her sister was not a baby," Jan says. "There is a twenty month difference in their ages. Gabriella is a dark-haired, dark-eyed version of her big sister. Katerina understood that she and Gabriella grew in their birth mother's tummy. She wondered, 'Will my other Mommy be at the orphanage?'"

"After the high expectations, the first time they saw each other was a disaster," Sherwood recalls. "We pulled up to the orphanage and parked in front of the walkway leading to the entrance. Standing on the walkway was a woman with a little child. Katerina looked out the window of the car and said, 'Daddy! That's my baby sister!' And I said, 'My goodness, yes it is, Honey.' I opened the car door and she bolted. She was a streak of lightening down that walkway. She threw her arms around her baby sister and Gabriella screamed and cried. She was terrified. Katerina had expected Gabriella to greet her with open arms. She sat down on the steps to the orphanage, her head in her hands, and sobbed."

Things turned around quickly. They spent the next hour at the orphanage. Katerina entertained her baby sister by doing somersaults and dances, trying to make her smile. She suc-ceeded. She also enjoyed climbing into Gabriella's crib. Gabriella bonded with Jan and Sherwood right away, but it took her a few weeks before she became attached to Katerina. Back at home, Katerina took on the role of protective big sister. "In the beginning, she was very possessive of Gabriella," Jan says. "Her possessiveness became quite a problem for a while, in terms of negative behavior to her friends, who wanted to befriend the adorable little girl. Katerina wanted to be the most important person in her baby sister's new life. Gabriella is also very protective and tender toward her sister. They've only been together five months and are already so connected. Both girls are extremely compassionate. They love music and dancing. One of their older sisters is an excellent singer, and has a beautiful voice. One of the brothers plays the guitar. Music is important to Romanians in general."

Sherwood's dream is that there will be four parents walking the girls down the aisle when they get married. He and Jan wish there were a way to directly connect with the birth family, but they haven't been able to open up that channel yet. Contact between families is not encouraged and the benefits of contact are not understood in Romania. "We would like to take the girls back sometime to meet their family, if the birth family wants that," Sherwood says. "We want to respect their feelings. They have asked for pictures. We know the village where they live. We know their names. In its time, it will happen."

CHARLIE CHRISTOPHER

"I FELL RIGHT INTO BECOMING THE STEREOTYPICAL BIRTH FATHER," FIFTY-five-year-old restaurateur Charlie Christopher confesses. "Get somebody pregnant and then disappear. Hope no one says anything."

The year was 1966. Charlie was a senior in college. "I was never the kind of guy who could meet someone in a bar for a one-night stand," he explains. "I always built up a relationship before dating or becoming intimate. After dating Lora for a while, it became clear that, in spite of her being a wonderful person, I was not ready to embark on a lifetime thing. I was about to graduate. I also needed to keep my distance. After being so hurt the summer before, I was too gun-shy to become emotionally involved with anyone."

The previous summer, Charlie's heart had been broken when a woman to whom he was engaged broke it off two weeks before their wedding. "My senior year, I was in a depressed state, and was drinking a lot on the weekends for 'medication.' But everyone was partying and drinking. We would tap the keg at noon on Friday. So it all seemed okay."

Charlie found out that his new girlfriend, Lora, was pregnant after they'd gone a month without speaking. "I felt that we were phasing out," he says. "At first, she wasn't going to tell me. I didn't know what to do. I just knew I couldn't marry her. A friend of mine had gotten married in a similar situation, and it was disastrous."

He already had an airplane ticket to visit Europe after graduation. After learning about Lora's pregnancy, Charlie was planning to never come back home. "I was just going to disappear because of the shame of it all," he says. "From time to time during the trip, I called my parents, and began to suspect they knew. I was right. While I was gone, Lora's father had called my father to tell him. It was difficult to think about facing the situation. I wasn't good at stuff like that."

When Charlie returned home that September, Lora was in her eighth month. "Her father had hidden her in an apartment on the outskirts of town to keep her pregnancy a secret," he recalls. "In those days, it was very shameful when a woman got pregnant out of wedlock." Charlie's father told him that he could not believe, with all of the available knowledge about contraception, how he could have let it happen. "He couldn't believe how irresponsible I was," Charlie says. "I saw his point. I was twenty-two, not fifteen. But when I look back, I don't think I had any of the tools to know what to do. My mother asked me why I didn't go to my father for help. If I thought I could have, I would have. There was something unspoken in our family that didn't allow me to be open with them. I felt like a failure. I had done this horrible thing and made everyone's life miserable. I was the bad guy."

Finally, Charlie went to see Lora and meet her parents. He wanted to accept responsibility. "At least in my father's eyes, by doing that I had faced the music a bit. That was some solace. It was a long time ago, but I can see the whole scene as if it were yesterday," he says. "I made it pretty clear that we weren't going to get married. That did not seem to be the answer, especially for the child. At this point, though, the baby was just a concept. I didn't think of the child as a person."

No one called Charlie when the baby was born. The first knowledge he had of his daughter's birth came when the relinquishment papers for her adoption arrived in the mail. "It seems so small of me, but in a way I felt relieved when I received the papers. I wasn't going to have to figure out what to do anymore. The voices inside me were saying this was best for the baby. A terrible thing had happened, but at least the child would have a great home, which I could not provide."

When Charlie married in 1970, he told his wife that he did not want to have children. "I had already done that," he explains. "I felt like those guys in 'Wayne's World,' the ones who always say 'I'm not worthy.' I felt like it was not okay for me to have more kids."

Charlie's wife helped him change his mind, and their daughter Alison was born in 1972. Cradling her in his arms, Charlie began to understand the depth of love that a parent could feel for a child and, at the same time, what it meant to give his first daughter away. "After Allison was born, I was woozy for weeks. It just hit me so hard what I had done," he recalls. "But I really looked at losing my first daughter as punishment for having been so irresponsible and bad. You give your child away, and as punishment, you never see her again. I was just bearing up under my 'sentence.' You rob a bank, you go to jail."

Another daughter, Ashley, was born in 1974, and again the power of Charlie's love for his new child overwhelmed him. Although his wife knew about the daughter he had relinquished before they married, "She didn't really get it," he says. "She didn't understand what a big thing it was for me. I frequently found myself alone out in the barn, weeping over those relinquishment papers. I was in despair and grief. I could not believe I gave my kid away."

In 1978, Charlie began contacting the adoption agency. "I had heard it was good for adoptees to have information available at the agency. The social worker said that only one other birth father had been in contact, and he never called again. I was the only other one in twenty years. I couldn't understand that. Perhaps it's because the birth father feels he really is the bad guy. I don't know how a birth father can feel any other way. The birth mother had to endure all she had to endure, and the baby is innocent. I wore that bad-guy sign quite well. If you can suppress it, maybe you're better off. That despair sets up house in a little corner of your soul, and it never goes

Charlie looking toward the Hudson River from the boat basin in New York City

away. It's always gnawing at you."

The social worker who had placed Charlie's daughter was still at the agency. "A week after we first talked, she called me," he recalls. "She told me she'd just seen my daughter, that she was in the sixth grade and looked happy. That felt good. I did the right thing. She was with nice people, having a regular life. I was so happy to know she was alive. I wanted to believe all the social worker said was true."

Over the next few years, Charlie continued talking with adoptees and realized that, although he felt he had done enough by sending a photograph and medical information to the agency, an adoptee may actually need to know much more about her birth parents. When his daughter turned twenty-one, Charlie began to search for her. For a long time, he tried various methods. He learned from the agency that the law had just changed in his state, and, whereas they would

first writing me, she went to my restaurant, unannounced, to try to check me out. After the call, we began writing back and forth."

The following June, father and daughter finally met. "I knew her from fifty yards away," Charlie recalls. "She looked just like Lora. When we hugged for the first time, it was just unbelievable. We spent from mid-afternoon until midnight catching up."

Learning about Jennifer's struggles was difficult for Charlie, since he took responsibility for the problems she'd had while growing up. "I just wish I could fix things for her. I'm a control freak and this is out of my control," he explains. "Since our reunion, we've had many wonderful times together. I've met her adoptive parents, and become close with her adoptive father. Jennifer and Lora have also met and developed a relationship. Knowing Jennifer has brought great changes to my life. But

---

"IT SEEMS SO SMALL OF ME, BUT IN A WAY I FELT RELIEVED WHEN I RECEIVED THE PAPERS. I WASN'T GOING TO HAVE TO FIGURE OUT WHAT TO DO ANYMORE. THE VOICES INSIDE ME WERE SAYING THIS WAS BEST FOR THE BABY."

---

have helped him before, they now could not. Charlie felt he had to let his daughter find out more about him if she wanted to. His search was all about what she might need. "When my attempts failed, I stapled two thousand dollars to a piece of cardboard and mailed it to a private investigator," he says. "Two days later, I found out who she was."

That was in June. It took Charlie until October to write his daughter a letter. "I didn't want to do the wrong thing again," he says. "Jennifer wrote back in November. Of course, I was ecstatic. Anything more from her was just going to be a bonus. I wrote back, and didn't hear from her again. A year later, she called. It was just amazing. I had to write down everything she said or it would have all washed right over me. She told me she had gone to the agency when she was sixteen, and met with the same social worker. She saw my picture and read my letter, which was in her file. That June after

the despair is still there. I can't imagine it not being there."

Since 1966, Charlie had had a recurring dream so vivid that, over time, he convinced himself it was real. "In my dream, I saw Jennifer when she was a week old. The baby was in a bassinet in Lora's apartment. I walked into that room, trying hard to feel disconnected from the child. Lora asked me if I wanted to hold her. I told her I didn't want to, because that would be trouble. I have grieved over that memory. Not only was I so bad to have given my child away—I had seen her first. But after Lora and I met as adults, I learned that the baby had never gone back to her apartment. I had never seen her. I had a really clear memory of something that actually never happened.

"The consequences of my choice will always be with me," Charlie reflects. "You don't get the option to rewrite the script. You don't get the chance to do that scene over."

When Penny Partridge was six years old, she asked her adoptive mother why she had been given up for adoption.

"Your mother was too poor to keep you," was her adoptive mother's reply.

At the time, Penny thought that the gardener who worked at her family's San Gabriel home would be considered poor, yet he and his wife managed to keep their children. She remembers thinking, "So either my mother was so poor she must have lived in a mud hut, or she hadn't loved me as much as the gardener and his wife love their children."

Not until the age of ten did Penny broach the subject again. She and her father were in the car running errands. "Daddy, I know my name was Dorothy Elizabeth before I was adopted. But what was my last name?" she asked. Her father began coughing and then slumped over the steering wheel. "I thought he was having a heart attack," she recalls.

Twenty years passed before Penny mentioned adoption to her father again. By this time, she was married with children, living in Philadelphia, and had co-founded the Adoption Forum to promote communication within the adoption community. Her mother was helping her search for her birth family. It was Christmas. Seated with her parents in the living room of their home in California, Penny reassured her father. "It's not that I want to replace you. I just want to see someone I look like."

Her father harumphed. "What if your birth mother's gone on and married a senator, and you arrive at their house in the middle of a cocktail party? You could ruin the man's career!"

Penny in the woods behind her home in Amherst, Massachusetts

"Daddy, you're my father!" cried Penny. "You're supposed to worry about me, not some man you don't even know."

He stood up and walked across the room with arms opened wide, tears in his eyes. "Oh, my dear, what can I do to help?" To Penny, that action made a profound difference. "All I needed from him was exactly what he was doing at that moment," she explained. "He was relating to me in a way I had never experienced. Perhaps it was the first time he knew in his heart that he was my real father. Opening up this subject gave me my father."

The search for her birth mother led Penny from Pipestone County, Minnesota, to the 1880 Census in the National Archives in Washington, D.C., to a seed company in South Dakota, where she tracked down one of her cousins. "When I made the first call, a man answered the phone. I said, 'Is this Mr. Callan?' and he said, 'Yes.' I said, 'I'm looking for a Mr. Callan who would have a sister named Catharine.' He said, 'Well, that would be my father.' And I said, 'How could I speak to your father?' He said, 'You can't. He died a few months ago.'

"So I asked if he had an aunt named Catharine, and he said, 'Yes, she lives in Cheyenne, Wyoming.' That was the first moment I knew my mother was alive. She was seventy-one years old. I hadn't missed knowing her."

When Penny discovered there was no phone listing for Catharine Callan, she called her cousin again. He told her that her birth mother had married, and that her husband had died, but that the phone would probably still be in his name. The number was listed exactly as her cousin suggested. Penny debated about whether to call that night or wait twenty-four hours. Deciding she would only become more nervous over time, she ate dinner, rehearsed what she was going to say, then dialed the number.

"I was so scared. It seemed as if I were on the ceiling, watching myself dialing. But hearing her voice, which seemed so down-to-earth, brought me back into my body again," she recalls.

Penny carefully spoke the words she had rehearsed. "This is Penny Partridge from Philadelphia," she said, "and the reason I'm calling is that I think we're related."

"Oh, you're joking," was her birth mother's response.

"But she knew exactly who I was," says Penny. "I told her where and when I had been born, and then I broke down and sobbed, 'I just want to meet you.' And she said, 'Oh, I thought this might happen. Would you like to come visit me?'

"We chose a time three weeks later when we were both available. My parents bought me my plane ticket to meet Catharine for the first time."

The day before Penny was to fly, a huge blizzard threatened to delay their reunion. The airport was closed. "Catharine called and said, 'Well, we've waited a long time to meet each other, and it looks like we're just going to have to wait some more.' But I knew that if I had to crawl through the snow from Denver to Cheyenne, I would not postpone this trip. Fortunately, they reopened the airport. The only time I heard Catharine sound at all nervous was when I called her to tell her that I was coming after all. She said, 'Oh, well, you're going to have to take me like I am.' I said, 'You're going to have to take me like I am, too.'"

The next day, Penny boarded a flight to Cheyenne. Then she took a cab to Catharine's home, which turned out to be a small white house. Through the picture window, she caught her first glimpse of her birth mother. "A little old lady was watching a huge television in a pine-paneled living room. That moment was the one time, in my entire search, that I thought, 'Do I want to do this? What am I doing?' It felt foreign to me."

As Penny approached the house, the taxi driver kicked ice away from the storm door to open it. Her birth mother stood framed in the doorway. The first moments were spent paying the driver and getting Penny's suitcase inside. "Finally we were alone. Catharine said, 'I'd kiss you, but I don't want to give you my cold,' and she kissed me on the cheek. Then we went in and sat down and she said, 'I don't know where to start.'

"We began to prepare dinner, and it was lovely, because she planned what she wanted to feed me for my first meal." At the dinner table, Penny noticed her birth mother's hand. "It was the most exciting moment of the whole visit. I saw my hand across the table on her body. What was my hand doing over there on her body? It was like a hallucination. I said, 'Oh, Catharine, look at our hands.' We put our hands together and they were almost identical. 'Yup, they're my Dad's hands. I've always liked my hands,' Catharine said.

"For me," Penny recalls, "the moment represented what I missed and what I needed, which was to see that my body came from someone. That I came from someone."

In the middle of dinner, Catharine jumped up and asked Penny to follow her. "We went into her bedroom and she started to show me photographs. 'These are your grandparents,' she said. I was amazed and grateful that she would let me think of them as my grandparents. Then Catharine opened her jewelry box and found an opal ring her parents had given her when she graduated from college. 'Try this on.' She wanted me to have it. It was a perfect fit. I felt like Cinderella."

Later that night, Penny lay exhausted in the bedroom across the hall from her birth mother's room. "I was drifting off to sleep when I heard her voice booming out, 'Well, was I anything like you expected?' I don't know today what I would say to that question. In some ways she was. I had expected Catharine to be an independent and feisty person, and she was. But she was also tender and sad. She felt the loss in a way I didn't. I had my childhood with my adoptive parents. She missed it. She had no other children. But for me, knowing the truth, whatever the reality, was so much better than having just fantasy.

"One of the biggest gifts she gave me was my conception story. Knowing it is one of the miracles of my life. The story is far more fantastical than anything I could have imagined.

"At forty, Catharine was a short, round school teacher from South Dakota. Billy Duckett was a tall, thin high school dropout from Arkansas. It was during World War II, and they were working for an American company looking for oil in the Northwest Territories of Canada near the Arctic circle. Catharine said that there was not much to do at night, unless you wanted to get up and watch the bears rummage through the garbage. She and Billy were the only employees who didn't like poker, so they quickly became friends.

"One night, Billy knocked on the door of Catharine's Quonset hut and said, 'Come on out, you have to see this.' They got in his truck and drove out of the company compound. There was a fabulous display of the aurora borealis, the northern lights. Catharine told me it was as if there were hundreds of dancers twirling across the sky with rainbow chiffon scarves. Electricity was crackling in the air. It felt like the two of them were alone in the universe. I was conceived that night, under that sky."

Today, Penny is in her fifties, an adoptive mother of two, and a poet. Many of her poems concern her experience and perspective as an adopted person. Some people refer to her as "the poet laureate of the adoption community."

To reflect her identity as a daughter of four parents, Penny has taken her birth mother's maiden name, Callan, as her middle name, and her adoptive parents' name, Partridge, as her last name. She wears two rings on her right hand. "One has been passed down through my adoptive family," she explains. "It's a jade-and-silver ring that my great-grandmother bought in China before World War I. On the next finger, I wear a solid gold ring that was given to my birth father by the company he and Catharine worked for in Canada. Beside the place and the year I was conceived are engraved the initials BPC, which stands for Bechtel Price Callahan, the name of the oil company. But I see the initials as standing for Billy, Penny, and Catharine.

"One's oval, one's round; one's silver, one's gold. They are very different rings, but they look good together."

"THE ADOPTED PERSON'S SEARCH FOR HIS ORIGINS IS A RELIGIOUS EXPE-
rience. It is a spiritual journey, a pilgrimage of self-knowledge, a holy endeavor."

Father Thomas Brosnan is a pastor of the Blessed Sacrament Church in Brooklyn,
New York. When he was six months old, he was adopted by an Irish couple from
Brooklyn. As a boy, he never saw himself as the result of a real union between a man and a
woman. "I used to watch Superman reruns every day. It was a ritual: turning on the TV and
secretly hoping they would replay that very first episode, when the infant Superman lands
on earth, ejected from faraway Krypton, only to be found in the open field by the kindly
Kents. Growing up, I literally felt alienated. I never saw myself as having been born."

Years later, as an adult, Father Tom had a dream that brought relief and revelation. "I
was in a sort of spa. It was steaming hot, and there were several whirlpools with hot,
sudsy water swirling around. The marble floors were slippery. Somehow, I knew that if I
entered one of the whirlpools, I would be sucked right down through the vortex. I felt
exhilaration and excitement as I entered, and felt myself going round and round, down
and down, as if in a tunnel speeding toward a veiled light. Then I woke up. I believe I
dreamt of my own conception. I really was born into this world then."

Father Tom, a timid only child, grew up in a small Brooklyn rowhouse with his adoptive parents and grandparents. "I was suffocated with good intentions and too much elderly company," he recalls. "At Thanksgiving, my parents set up the table in the living room,
and it would go all the way into my grandparents' bedroom. The table ran almost the

whole length of the house, but there were never any other kids."

At the age of five, Tom discovered he had been adopted when he overheard a conversation. "We never talked about it," he recalls, "yet looking back now, it seems it was the very air we breathed."

His grandmother had warned Tom's mother never to tell him he was adopted. "She believed things would never be the same," he says. "During the summer when we'd go to the beach, although I had platinum blond hair, I got a deep tan. My parents were Irish and they just burned. My grandmother used to wash me in the sink, scrubbing and scrubbing my skin. When my mother asked why she was scrubbing so hard, she'd say, 'I'm just trying to get the dirt off.'"

A young priest, one of Tom's favorite teachers, advised his parents to tell him he was adopted. "I remember the day they told me. I was twelve years old, and I'd just come home from school. My mother tried, but gave up and passed the task to my poor father. He explained awkwardly that they had adopted me because they were infertile. My mother asked if I had any questions. I didn't, so we went out to lunch. I fell into a deeper silence about myself in the face of her discomfort. I felt shame about being adopted."

Since he was very young, Father Tom had wanted to become a Catholic priest. He felt at home with the rituals, the Latin, the candles and incense, the churches themselves. "As I sought support and acceptance for who I was, I made the church my parent. I could not take off my shirt and reveal the "S" anywhere else.

"When you feel out of place, you can't announce yourself fully to the world. I carry both the feeling of belonging and not belonging. Secrets robbed me of intimacy with others and with myself. For me, life and love are intertwined with the experience of loss. In a strange way, I feel more comfortable in places I don't belong."

In fact, it was during several trips to Korea as an adult, to learn the language and culture in order to work with Korean immigrants in his parish, that Father Tom became powerfully aware of his need to search for his birth family. "Korea was so foreign. For the first time in my life, I could identify those feelings of displacement as something I had always known, but had somehow grown used to. This lonely period was a revelation. As I was learning to speak Korean, I was also learning to interpret my life through the metaphor of exile, of emigrant, of pilgrim, of searcher. Traveling to the other side of the world and living with culture shock ignited something in me—a deeply felt need to search for my birth mother."

Father Tom will never forget the day he walked into the Catholic Home Bureau in Manhattan to ask for information about his adoption. "I went to the agency dressed as a priest and sat before Sister Una, the nun in charge. She gave me my non-identifying information, all the information I could have that would not lead me directly to my birth mother, and the whole time she was so condescending. 'Now, Father. Why would you want to know? Did you have a bad adoption?' she asked me. I wanted to kill her."

Father Tom discovered that, after the death of her father, his birth mother Casey lived for a time with her stern mother and younger brother in the servants' quarters of a physician's home in suburban Philadelphia. To escape her mother's strictness, she moved to Baltimore to be near her older brother, a Jesuit priest and the apple of their mother's eye. There, Casey moved into a boarding house affiliated with the Peabody Conservatory of Music, and fell in love with a student from Toronto. After he returned home, she discovered she was pregnant. She traveled to Toronto to plead with him to marry her. He refused, for religious reasons. Back in Baltimore, she revealed her dilemma to another music student, a young man from Virginia who offered to marry her. Within a few weeks, however, the wedding was called off. Casey finally confided in her brother, who arranged for her to go to a Catholic maternity home in New York City. Her

Father Tom in The Blessed Sacrament Church (Brooklyn, New York)

Baltimore roommate, Sophia, was the only one to know.

While searching for his birth mother, Father Tom discovered that her older brother had subsequently moved to Georgetown, and had died rather young. His name was also Tom. "One day, I got into my car and drove down to Georgetown," says Father Tom. "I visited my uncle's grave and decided to ring the bell at the Jesuit residence. The priest who answered turned out not only to have been my uncle's classmate, but also his best friend. I spent the entire day with him, listening to stories of their friendship. After dinner, he invited me to his room to see some old photos. As we were about to open the album, it dawned on me that this would be the first time in my life that I was going to see someone related to me."

In 1985, Father Tom reunited with his birth mother. "She did not want me to find her," he says. "She felt there were too many complications and too much to explain. It took her a year, yet once she finally told her other six children, I was always included in family functions, at her insistence. At first, I think she was worried that they might think less of her. After a year of meeting clandestinely, we arranged for me to meet the rest of the family. Shortly before that day, she had an asthma attack. The hospital released her for the meeting. We were all in the living room together, and it was wonderful. They asked her questions I could never bring myself to ask."

As for Father Tom's birth father, he still denies paternity, and refuses to have a blood test. In their one conversation, his father had many questions about Casey. It was clear to Father Tom that he had cared about her.

"A blood test is not really necessary to confirm paternity," says Father Tom. His love of languages—he studied nine and speaks five—led him to believe that he had indeed talked to his birth father. "Whatever language I happened to be studying, I'd fantasize it was the language that fit my background. I wonder about the genetics of language. I especially loved studying Russian, and my teacher, a Ukrainian immigrant, asked me several times if I were Russian, because my accent

was near perfect. I'd say, 'No, Irish,' not wanting to admit I didn't know where I came from. As it turns out, my birth father was born in Poland."

The Sunday after Easter, Father Tom was reflecting on the story of the risen Jesus appearing to his disciples. The disciple Thomas was absent, and because of his refusal to believe the story, he is referred to as Doubting Thomas. "I'll never believe it," the disciple tells them, "without probing the nail prints in His hands, without putting my fingers in the nail-marks and my hand into His side."

"That story resonates with me," says Father Tom. "It's a graphic story, and could, I suppose, be considered vulgar. To probe the wounds of someone's body is gross. Thomas did not want to settle for a belief in ghosts. Others may prefer it, but he wanted nothing to do with disembodied spirits. Jesus invites Thomas to explore His body. 'Thrust your hands into my wound,' He says. 'Do not persist in your unbelief, but believe.'

"Adoptees are in search of missing bodies, alive or dead. We need a 'hands-on' experience. We are tired of having to believe in ghosts. The disciple Thomas is actually filled with courage—the courage to doubt, and to question. He had the courage to search for real bodies, bodies that signify real wounds, real experiences of loss and the desire to belong.

"The adopted person is a sacrament, the sanctifying grace of every man's search to find that holy ground wherein the fusion of nature and grace is manifest, the search for that sacred place where sex and love have intercoursed."

Since his birth mother's death, ten years after their reunion, Father Tom has met her former roommate, Sophia. "The last time, she brought me a gift. It was a photograph she found by accident, a picture of my mother and father cheek to cheek, posing in one of those quick picture booths. As I studied their faces, I secretly wondered whether I was there too, still unseen, or about to enter the vortex of that whirlpool in my dream, forever, from then on, a part of their lives."

ONE HOT, STEAMY TEXAS AFTERNOON, WHEN HE WAS ABOUT THREE YEARS old, Larry Baker's mother led him down the long, dark hall to her bedroom. "I remember her saying, 'Your father's home. Why don't you come in and see him?' Now, I was used to sleeping in my mother's bed. I can still remember the feeling of lying next to her. There was my father, lying in what I considered my bed, propped up with pillows against the headboard. The sheet was pulled up to his waist. A pair of binoculars hung around his neck. 'How you doin' there, boy?' he asked. This is my first memory of my father.

"Decades later, I asked him why he was wearing binoculars. There was no punch line. He said he was just looking out the window."

Larry's father was rarely home. "Even when he was around the house, he never spoke to my two older brothers and me. He never touched us. He never acknowledged our presence. My last three years at home coincided with his retirement from the military after thirty-three years. He was cold, angry, and sullen. Sometimes he drank too much, and he stayed away from home as much as he could—not on a daily basis, but enough to shape a fifteen year-old's sense of his father."

At nineteen, Larry became a father himself. "I never held my son, Tim. I have no real memory of him when he was a baby. Just as no man had ever touched me when I was growing up, my son had no physical contact with me at all. I was cold, angry, and sullen, the exact duplicate of my father. My marriage was doomed to failure, and my

Four year-old Larry stands between his brothers (and in front of father)

son got caught in the middle. He came to live with me when he turned seven. Until he was thirteen, it was just him and me. I treated him like a roommate or a younger brother. I dragged him to parties. I didn't try at all to be a parent. I was convinced that I was not meant to have children. My second wife, Ginger, changed all that. I will forever owe her."

Ginger felt that Larry and Tim were so antagonistic toward each other that their relationship was only going to get worse. After she and Larry married, Tim went to live with Larry's mother.

By this time, both Ginger and Larry were in their late thirties, and didn't plan to have children because they felt they were too old. So Larry had a vasectomy. "They claimed it would feel no worse than a bee sting," he recalls. "They said I'd be able to go horseback riding the next day. No! I had every complication possible."

A few years later, her mother's death caused Ginger to reconsider parenthood, and she approached Larry about having children. "I figured the worst that could happen is that we'd have kids and they'd be her kids," he says. "Parenthood still meant nothing to me. I went ahead and had a vasectomy reversal. At the time that procedure required a two-day hospital stay.

"That first year of trying to get pregnant was the worst year of our marriage. The strain was too much. Ginger approached me about adoption, and I still felt it was just for her."

After attending a few meetings, Larry and Ginger learned that the social service agencies had restrictions about parents' ages, and that they were too old to get an infant. "Then we found the Holt Agency, which handled foreign adoptions from Korea," Larry says. "Their most difficult question for prospective parents was, 'Would it bother you if your children wouldn't look like you?' It didn't bother me, because I still didn't think I'd consider them my children. I was not being truthful with Ginger about my feelings. I don't think she understood how indifferent I was to parenting again. And I don't think I understood how much parenting meant to her.

"So you've got two adults who are pushing forty, each with familial baggage that they've carried all their lives, thinking they are going to be parents. As the ten-month process began, I first followed Ginger's lead, and then I finally began to look forward to having a child. I didn't step in feet first, but I leaned forward, and the feet followed."

Larry realized that adopting involves a much more collaborative effort than giving birth to a baby. Other people must be depended on to make adoption happen. The Holt Agency required that he and Ginger write individual autobiographies, and talk about their own parents and spouses. "The process began to transform me into a parent, especially as I began to understand my relationships with my father and my son Tim.

"Also, I realized that one of the great things about becoming adoptive parents is that the mother doesn't have an exclusive experience with the child the way biological mothers do during the pregnancy," Larry continues. "Neither one of us was physically connected. So we both experienced an emotional bonding rather than a physical one. We were on equal footing."

At first, he and Ginger had hoped for a girl. "I wanted a girl for a very specific reason," Larry says. "I had a son. How would Tim feel if I had another son after failing him? Also, Ginger wondered if I would repeat the same mistakes I had made with him."

Two weeks later, the agency sent them photographs of Ben, and Larry reconsidered his position on the gender issue. "I really thought this could be my kid. All of a sudden, there was a real person out there who was waiting for us," Larry says. "The agency only needed one word—yes or no—and the baby was ours. And so began the subtle process of becoming a part of that person, and that person becoming a part of yourself."

The agency arranged to have the Korean babies flown to the United States, accompanied by social workers. After spending the night in California, the babies continued on to their new adoptive homes. At ten o'clock on the night before four month-old Ben was to arrive, Larry and Ginger were mixing formula when the phone rang. They learned that Ben was not on the plane. He would arrive a week later.

"The next weekend, Ginger and I were very cool. We were not about to let go and get excited again," Larry remembers. "We had to drive a hundred miles to the airport in Des Moines. When we got there, we were told the plane had gotten as far as Denver, and was snowed in. So we spent the night in a flea-bag motel and went to the movies."

The next day, the plane finally arrived. "In preparation, I had shaved off my beard, because Koreans don't have facial hair, and some children react to beards," explains Larry. The agency had asked each family to bring their own blanket to wrap the baby in, because of the inevitable chaos when babies come off the plane. "Six babies were on the flight. Six social workers, with blankets gathered from the six waiting adoptive families, boarded the plane. The deplaning passengers were reacting in one of two ways: either irritably, 'I've just been on a plane with six crying babies!'; or holding back, to see what happened when the babies came out," Larry recalls.

"An airline employee walked up to the group of adoptive parents and announced, 'They're coming.' I remember Ginger saying it felt like that scene in a delivery room, where the doctor announces, 'I see the head!', and the baby is born," Larry says. "As the babies began to come off the plane one by one, I felt this swell. I'd been told that this is the way fathers feel when they attend the birth of their child. When Ben was placed in my arms, I knew that feeling, finally."

At first, Ginger worked full time, and Larry was the stay-at-home parent. He would hold Ben in one arm for hours, sitting in a rocking chair, while writing his doctoral dissertation with the other. When Ben was eighteen months old, they adopted through the Holt Agency again. Like Ben, Jenny arrived when she was four months old.

"Looking back, I'm not surprised at the way Ginger has evolved as a mother," says Larry. "I'm just surprised at how I've become a father. We are both trying to create a childhood for our kids that we didn't have. I did not understand the full impact my father had on me until Ben and Jenny 'grew up with me.' That is why I'm so self-conscious about parenting them. Children absorb so much from how their parents act, much more than from what they say. And so we dote on them, and they probably think we hug them too much!"

By becoming a genuine father, Larry believes, he has become a better husband. "The children are a strong bond between us. You're willing to give up your existence for your children," he says. "Would I give up my last kidney for my children? Yes. Would Ginger give up her last kidney for me? Would I do it for her?" Larry quipped. "Well, no. But we will make each other's graves look very nice and tend the flowers." He and Ginger love to joke with each other. But, he remembers, "There was no laughter in my house when I was growing up. I never got the sense that my parents were in love, never saw them touch, or even laugh together."

At his mother's funeral, Larry did not shed a tear. "I would like the saddest moment of my children's lives to be when their parents die, unless of course they were to lose their own child or spouse. That would be the worst. But if they feel toward us the way we feel toward them, it will be one of the saddest moments of their lives. My son, Tim, was genuinely touched by his grandmother's death. He felt about her the way I should have felt about her."

Larry will grieve when his father passes away. "I will apologize at his funeral, admit I had been too harsh on him, and that there were missed opportunities. I might even get misty-eyed. I know nothing about my father's life, and he's too old to pull it up now. He's never been a talker, and he's not a contemplative person. But I want Ben and Jenny to know all about their parents' lives, especially what we did before they were born.

Baker family gathering on the porch in their home (Iowa City, Iowa)

"I am interested in meeting their birth fathers. I would love to see what they look like and who they are, and how that shows up in Ben and Jenny. I think I would look at the birth fathers as a version of who I was, as the absent father I was in my first marriage, as my own father was in my childhood. I could say, 'You don't know what you missed.' Even if the birth fathers have other children, they missed parenting this particular child, and that's their loss."

After writing short stories for thirty years, Larry wrote his first novel, *The Flamingo Rising*, which Hallmark is developing into a TV-movie. The novel begins, "My name is Abraham Isaac Lee, and I am my father's son."

"I, too, am my father's son," Larry says. "It took a long time for me to write a book about parental love, because I never felt parental love as a child, and never gave it as an adult to my son Tim. I never felt parental until we adopted Ben and Jenny. *The Flamingo Rising* would not exist if they had not come into my life.

"The first paragraph on the acknowledgments page of my book is an apology to my son Tim. 'To those I have hurt or disappointed in my past, I am sorry. Especially to Tim, who deserves better than he got.'"

From Left: Cathy, Matthew, and Brenda at the family campground (Elk Lake, Michigan)

THE CRYSTAL-CLEAR AQUA WATERS OF ELK LAKE IN MICHIGAN REVEAL ITS sandy bottom. A float for diving and sunning sits offshore. Row boats drift, tied to a nearby dock. The fragrance of damp woods mixes with the faint sweet scent of burnt marsh-mallow bits left on the brick grill, from the last time s'mores were cooked over an open fire. Four musty wood cabins with screened-in porches and yellow bug lights are scat-tered about the rustic campground. All combine to evoke childhood memories for an extraordinary gathering of two families brought together by one child, fourteen year-old Matt Lundy.

Matt's adoptive parents, Cathy and Doug Lundy, and his sister, Nicole, own and oper-ate the campground. Every summer, they invite Matt's other family—his birth mother Brenda, her husband Clemens, their children Katarina and Daniel, and the whole extended family—to spend a week with them. Over these seven light-hearted days, Brenda asks the children questions like, 'What is your favorite color?' and 'What's your favorite memory of the previous year?' Then she records their answers in family albums.

All year long, Aunt Maureen, Brenda's sister, collects bits of chains and colored beads for the girls, who gather around a picnic table to create sparkling bracelets and neck-laces. Clemens loves paddling around the lake in a rowboat, filled with the younger chil-dren in their yellow and orange life jackets. Matt plays golf with his adoptive father and his grandfather Mike, Brenda's dad, who made Matt his first set of clubs.

"Some people say Matt will grow up confused by knowing his birth family," Brenda says. "During my pregnancy, I considered Matthew my child. I rubbed my belly and poked, and he kicked back. I held the Walkman to my belly and played Mozart. I talked to him and told him why I was placing him with his adoptive parents. Like any mother, I tried to protect him from being hurt. I kept myself from upsetting situations so my sense of peace would transfer to him. I told him I enjoyed being part of him. I prepared for the moment of surrender, the loss I would experience, in a similar way to how I prepared for the death of patients at the hospice where I worked."

Although Matt's birth father, Bayard, shared a deep friendship with Brenda, "We weren't romantically involved, so my expectations were different," she says. "I didn't expect him to be a knight in shining armor and rescue me."

Because Bayard lived three thousand miles away, Brenda knew he was not going to be a consistent father in their child's life. "I'm a strong person, and I can handle most things," she says. "But it was painful and humbling to come to the conclusion that I was not the best thing for Matthew. I felt he deserved two loving, stable people to raise him."

In the beginning of the adoption process, Brenda worked with an agency that offered semi-open adoptions. She was given a list of pre-adoptive couples to choose from; each couple's profile included five pieces of information such as occupation, number of years married, and religious affiliation. Once the adoption was final, there would be no further contact. "Luckily, in my seventh month, I read an article about an agency that offered open adoptions where the adoptive family and birth family know each other, and keep in contact," she recalls. "I called the head of the agency the next day and set the wheels in motion. After we met, he sent me seven profiles of prospective adoptive parents he felt I would like, given what he knew about me. He said he knew I would pick Doug and Cathy. Now, normally when someone tells me I am going to do something, I do everything in my power not to do it. But this decision was too important to let my pride get in the way.

I knew immediately that Doug and Cathy were the parents I wanted for my child."

Brenda first met Cathy and Doug when they came to her parents' home. During their visit, each of Brenda's brothers and sisters showed up 'unexpectedly' and circled the table where they were sitting. While Cathy was a little nervous, Doug talked and made jokes. "Doug's personality is a lot like mine," notes Brenda. "It was comforting to know that my child would have a parent with the same off-center sense of humor as me."

The hardest night of Brenda's life was the night before Doug and Cathy came to the hospital to pick up Matthew. "I was remaking the decision, going through all the gut-wrenching realizations again. After he was born, seeing him as a separate little person and taking care of him was really important to me. That was my time to be his mom. I couldn't place him with Doug and Cathy until I claimed him as my son. Cathy told me she knew that if I could leave the hospital without him, I wouldn't change my mind. She was right about that."

Brenda's mother, Teenie, a surgical nurse, was with Brenda when she was discharged from the hospital. Teenie wheeled her daughter, who was holding the baby, to the hospital door. Brenda asked the nurse who accompanied them to give the baby to Cathy. Cathy took the baby in her arms. Brenda and Teenie then walked away to their car and Doug and Cathy, with the baby, walked in the opposite direction. "I dissolved," Brenda remembers. "Cathy looked back, and I could tell she wanted to take a step toward me. She had a helpless look on her face. She wanted to do something to help me, but there was nothing she could do."

The first six months after Matthew's birth were very difficult. "Every night I woke up hearing his cries," Brenda recalls. "I would be halfway out of bed before I realized he wasn't there." When Matthew was three weeks old, she drove to Traverse City to sign papers in court. The judge stressed the finality of her decision. Even though all three were committed to an open adoption, legally Brenda had no rights. They had to trust one another. Doug and Cathy invited Brenda and her mother to spend that night at their house. "I couldn't stay there," Brenda recalls. "I was afraid that Matthew was going to cry in the middle of the night and I would just have to lie there and listen, not be able to get up to hold or comfort him. Now I know Cathy would not have minded at all. They know their children can love lots of people and it won't lessen the love they receive. She and Doug often say, 'You don't possess your children, you nurture them.'"

For Brenda, the first months after giving up Matthew were ones of grieving. "Those months were an endless treadmill of feeling horrible, not knowing why, and thinking I had no right to feel bad," Brenda recalls. "Open adoption is often viewed as not losing anything. I told the agency director, 'It's been two months and I feel like I lost him yesterday. Why, when I can

When Brenda married Clemens, she told him she didn't want any more children. "I filled our house with furniture, and it still seemed empty," she recalls. "To my horror, I realized what the house was missing was children. I began to realize that my shame about giving up Matthew was causing me to feel I wasn't worthy of having another child. What kind of mother material was I, after all? Rationally I knew why I placed him, but emotionally I felt I wasn't good enough. It took therapy to see myself differently."

Matt was eight years old when Brenda's daughter Katarina was born. "When I called Matt to tell him," she recalls, "the first thing he said was that he wanted a picture of my father holding the baby. He said, 'I want to see if he looks at her the same way he looks at me.'"

"On one of our recent family vacations at Elk Lake, Matt seemed to revel in the chance to be with my loud, large, bois-

---

"EVERY NIGHT I WOKE UP HEARING HIS CRIES," BRENDA RECALLS. "I WOULD BE HALFWAY OUT OF BED BEFORE I REALIZED HE WASN'T THERE."

---

see him anytime?' He helped me realize that I had lost being 'Matthew's mom.' I was not going to be the one he comes to throughout his life when he's hurt, when he has problems. I needed to grieve that I was not going to be that person for my son. Defining the loss helped me to move forward with the dificult process of grieving. A few months later, I stopped hearing Matthew crying at night. But about once a month until he was seven, I had dreams of being responsible for him and losing him."

Her parents, Mike and Teenie, also struggled. Originally, Mike did not want to hold Matt or get close to him, only to have him taken away, and never to see him again." My parents didn't visit Matthew until he was eleven months old," Brenda recalls. "My dad was afraid that Matt would never know him as his grandfather. Luckily, Matt took to him right away. When he was little, he literally followed my father around everywhere he went. He'd even wait outside the bathroom door."

terous family—a contrast to Doug and Cathy, who are quieter. As we were packing at the end of the week and the vacation was winding down, Matt reflected, 'I think I would be a different person if I had grown up in your family.' My gut reaction was to say, 'But look at the great kid you've become!' I wanted to say something that would take away the hurt in his voice. Instead I said, 'I wonder, too, what kind of person you would have been.'"

Matthew's birth father Bayard, who does stand-up comedy on the side, sent a tape of himself performing his comedy routine. "Matthew memorized parts of it and imitated Bayard perfectly," Brenda recalls. "It is so weird. They move alike. They talk alike. The first time my husband met Bayard, he couldn't stop laughing. He said, 'He is a grown-up Matthew!' Matthew looks like me and my grandfather, but he is so much like Bayard. I'm not sure if people who aren't adopted can be aware of how important it is to know who you look like, who

Front row: Katarina, Clemens, Brenda, Matthew, and Daniel. Back row: Cathy, Nicole and Doug

you sound like, who you act like, and where you get all of the things that make you who you are. There isn't a question he has asked that can't be answered.

"When Matthew was around three years old, he began understanding that he didn't grow in his mommy's tummy, that he came from me," Brenda continues. "He said to me, 'I was your baby while I was in the hospital, and then I became my mom and dad's baby when they took me home.' I said, 'Yes, that's right.' Then Matthew said, 'You must have been very sad.' I told him, 'Yes, I was very sad. And, in many ways, I'm still sad. The day you were born was one of the happiest and saddest days of my life, because I knew you weren't going to be with me for much longer. But I couldn't believe I was a part of making something so beautiful.' I feel I need to be the one saying these things to him."

"Matthew and I were going through his 'memory book'

recently. We were looking at the 'special visits' page, and he pointed to the photographs of me from when he was seven months old," Brenda says. "He asked why that was a special visit. And I told him it was the first time I had seen him since he was three weeks old. Matt asked me why I waited so long to see him for the first time. I began to tell him that I had been having a hard time, that I had just lost my job, when he said, 'I was a baby. I'm sure I didn't care if you had a job.' I'm glad I'm here to answer his difficult questions.

"Matthew may see himself mirrored in his birth parents, but he still is able to know that Doug and Cathy are his only parents. We are a blended family. Someone once said the greatest gift that parents can give their child is to love one another. I believe this carries over to open adoption. The greatest gift adoptive parents and birth parents can give their child is to love, honor, and respect one another.

"I LOST A LOT TO HAVE THIS LIFE IN AMERICA," SAYS ERIKA MANDER. NOW twenty-one and a drama student at Temple University, Erika was born in war-torn El Salvador. After their mother died when Erika was two years old, her oldest sister Rosa brought her two sisters and brother to the local orphanage. The family lived in extreme poverty, and their aunts and uncles could not afford to take care of all the children.

A long period of guerrilla warfare between right-wing and left-wing factions kept the country in political turmoil until 1992. "Soldiers lived in a military facility right by the orphanage," Erika remembers. "Sometimes there were riots outside. We were always hearing about kids whose limbs were blown off by mines. My mother used to prepare food for the soldiers. I think that is how she got pregnant a couple of times."

At the orphanage, run by nuns, the children attended school, and slept in one large room with many beds. Two lay women came in each day to take care of them. Only ten percent were truly orphans. Basically, the orphanage provided twenty-four-hour day care for mothers who could not take care of their children at home. The mothers visited on weekends.

When Erika was small, various people expressed interest in adopting her. But Rosa thought Erika would be too young to remember her siblings if she were taken from them too soon. "When my sisters felt I was old enough to never forget them, they allowed me to be adopted," Erika says. "I was ten. My sister Jakqueline was eighteen and leaving the orphanage. Rosa had already left. So I would be alone there. To prepare me for being

73

adopted, I was given a photo book of my new home, my new room, and my new mother. The house looked like a rich person's home. Jakqueline asked me to always think about her and Rosa and our brother, George, who was in a separate orphanage for boys. Jakqueline was very religious. We prayed a lot together. I loved her so much."

Jakqueline went with Erika and the social worker to meet her adoptive mother, Lynn Mander, at the airport. "Lynn was the only white person there," Erika remembers. "We loaded the car with boxes of stuff she brought for the orphanage. I didn't speak any English and she spoke only a little Spanish. She understood the language, but she really couldn't speak it. So we sat in the back seat and smiled at each other."

Lynn recalls, "I actually started talking about adopting when I was in high school in Chicago. Somehow I just knew that's what I wanted. I was working on Wall Street when I finally felt financially stable enough to follow through with my dream. Then Dean Witter offered me a job in Philadelphia, which I happily accepted."

Lynn began working with Lutheran Child Services of Philadelphia, which allows single parents to adopt. "They called me on my fortieth birthday and said, 'We have a little girl who is ten years old today and she is from El Salvador.' We have the same birthday."

Lynn's friends, Mary Beth and Andy, helped her pack for her trip to El Salvador. She was entering the country at the height of the civil war, and they were worried about her safety. "They told me to pack extra underwear, because I was going to s—— my pants when I got off the plane," Lynn says with a laugh.

She was sitting on the packages for the orphanage when the social worker brought Erika and Jakqueline to meet her. "Erika had on a red dress and looked just like her pictures," Lynn remembers. The social worker dropped Erika and her new mother off at the hotel. "It all was shocking to me," recalls Erika. "I had never stayed at a hotel and hardly ever ate in restaurants. We went to visit my brother at his orphanage and took him out to dinner. That was hard because he wanted to be adopted, too, and he was upset that I was leaving. On our last day in El Salvador, Lynn met my other sister, Rosa, and we all went to the airport. I don't remember seeing the airplane. I don't remember leaving. I don't remember saying good-bye.

"It was so cold when we arrived in Philadelphia. I was put into school right away, and the kids laughed at me at first because I could not speak English. My mom got my hair cut. I did whatever my mom wanted me to do."

Erika had heard stories about children being sent back to the orphanage if they didn't behave, so she tried to be very good. "We were told by the nuns not to cry or we would be sent back," she remembers. "I mostly got sad at night. I missed my family. Jakqueline gave me a silver medal with blue glass of the Virgin Mary that I held onto a lot. I never told Mom how hard it was for me."

Lynn had no idea what it was like for Erika to leave her family. "She was going through a lot, but I didn't pick up on it," Lynn says. "She was acting like the perfect child. We spent hours together each night on homework. It took a year, but eventually she could hold her own in school. We became very close. Erika and I were a poster family for the adoption agency. The agency gave out my phone number, and people called me to talk about adoptions of older children. I would go on and on about how easy it was."

In fact, everything had been so easy with Erika that Lynn wanted to adopt another child. When she asked Erika how she felt about it, she did not seem to care one way or the other. The call about Iris came when Erika and Lynn were in her office, on their way to a Whitney Houston concert in Madison Square Garden. "The agency told us that Iris was with her mother, but was available for adoption. I remember Erika saying, 'You can't do that. You can't take someone from their mother.' I told her it was not my decision to have Iris be

Iris, Lynn and Erika in their hammock (Wayne, Pennsylvania)

Family in Erika's bedroom

available for adoption. It was Iris's mother's choice."

Iris, who was eight at the time, wishes she had been a little older when she was adopted. "I would have been able to understand everything better. I have certain little memories of things in El Salvador. I remember taking care of my little brother and sister, Gepito and Eliza, when my mother went out to sell the pupusas and tamales we cooked together. My mother and I worked side by side, flattening dough into tortillas, stuffing them with cheese and spiced shredded pork. Then we folded and dry-fried them on a sheet of metal over an open fire. Gepito, Eliza, and I were the youngest of nine kids. The other brothers and sisters were much older. My mother was a really strong person, and that's the way I am. She kept us all fed and happy, most of the time, even though there wasn't a steady man in her life to help."

Iris remembers her mother telling her that by being adopted, she had an opportunity to go to the United States and get an education. Her mother wanted her to forget the horrors of war that she had been exposed to. Better memories would

mean a better life. "My mother said I would miss everyone. I would miss her. I was so angry that I yelled, 'No, I won't! I will never miss you again!' But things change. I was mad."

Her social worker held Iris's hand while they waited at the airport for her new American mother. Iris held flowers. After a few days, she and Lynn left for the United States. "Boarding the huge plane was scary," she recalls. "Planes drop bombs from the sky, so the thought of being inside one was terrifying. The first time I ever saw a toilet that flushed was on the plane."

Iris was drawn-looking and tiny. At eight years old, she was forty-two pounds, the size of a three-year-old. "She would get so sick to her stomach," Lynn recalls. "It took a long time to get her digestive system working. She talked eighty miles an hour in 'street Spanish,' had never been to school, and didn't even recognize her own name in writing. It had been so different with Erika. When she came, it wasn't long before we were able to read stories and play games together. But until Iris learned to communicate, I had no idea what she was interested in. It was difficult to know how to relate to her."

For the first year, Iris slept in a sleeping bag in Lynn's bedroom, because she was not used to having a room of her own. "I was scared to be in my own bed," she remembers. "I stayed up nights and cried because I missed my mother. I made sure Lynn and Erika knew that I missed my mother."

"Iris used to tell me about her family," Erika recalls. "She was scared a lot. Sometimes she thought she saw the ghost of her mother. That was freaky." Erika began feeling jealous of the attention Iris required. "My Mom and I were so close. For four years it was just the two of us, and now she spent a lot of time with Iris. In El Salvador, I was the baby in the family. I had older sisters. Now I was supposed to be Iris's older sister? How could I be her sister when I already had sisters, and I was missing them?"

Lynn cries as she remembers expecting the adjustment to be harder for Iris, since she missed her mother. She still had no idea about the pain Erika was going through. But when

Erika saw that Iris was not sent back to El Salvador for crying, she finally felt safe enough to begin talking about the physical and emotional abuse she had endured in the orphanage. The first year, as Iris slowly began to adjust to school and make friends, Erika was in and out of hospitals struggling with depression. Lynn's world turned upside down. She went from believing they were the perfect family to fearing she was going to lose Erika. Suddenly, she was the mother of two girls who were in a great deal of pain.

Although physically they could not look more different, Iris feels she and Lynn are very much alike. "We have the same personality, the same allergies. We think alike. We both have a good business sense. Erika is more artistic and likes to take her time doing things. We are very different people. Even now I can't say, 'That's my sister' to my friends. I just say, 'That's Erika.' When you bring children from different families over here, you can't expect them to like each other right away. It's beyond normal sister-to-sister disagreements. We don't fight at all. If Erika comes into a room, I leave. If I come into a room, she leaves. You can't expect kids to have perfect child-hoods because they are adopted. It's not the reality. It takes years, if ever. For Erika and me, there is still little connection and it's been seven years."

Erika has visited El Salvador three times. "Each time was worse," she says. "The last two visits, I felt guilty leaving my brother and sisters. I have a car, school, clothes. They don't have any of those luxuries. I spent all my money on them when I was down there. Mom said, 'You are the younger person, you shouldn't be taking care of them.' But what do you do when you have so much and they don't? I bought them pants, T-shirts, shoes for the kids, books for school. We went to McDonald's a lot. That was a big deal for my nieces and nephews. Over the years, I've had many letters from them. It's not fair that I wasn't there. Maybe if I had stayed, I could have changed the way things turned out. It's hard being away from your family.

"But at the same time," she continues, "Lynn is the only mother I've ever known. I love her so much. I still find myself trying to please her in every way. I would never change what has happened to me. My life makes me who I am. I'll keep it all, good or bad."

Iris, now fifteen, feels differently about her native country. "I would love to see my mother and my family again. But I don't want to be back in that land. There is so much more to the world. I used to see my mother and stepfather in dreams. But I haven't thought about seeing my mother again. I have so much I want to do, so much I want to conquer, and goals I want to meet. Maybe when I get older. Right now, I'm not sure I have the strength to do it."

Iris finds it difficult to explain to her friends all she is feeling about the difference between her life in the United States and her memories of living in El Salvador. "If I tell a friend I built my own home because the old one burned, they think of a house like theirs, not a cardboard box house like the one I used to live in. If I talk about war, all they know is the movie *Saving Private Ryan*. Sometimes it's hard for me not to flip out on them. They can be so self-centered. If they point to a homeless man downtown, I say, 'You wouldn't want anyone pointing at you if you were in that situation.' They haven't learned yet that the world doesn't revolve around them."

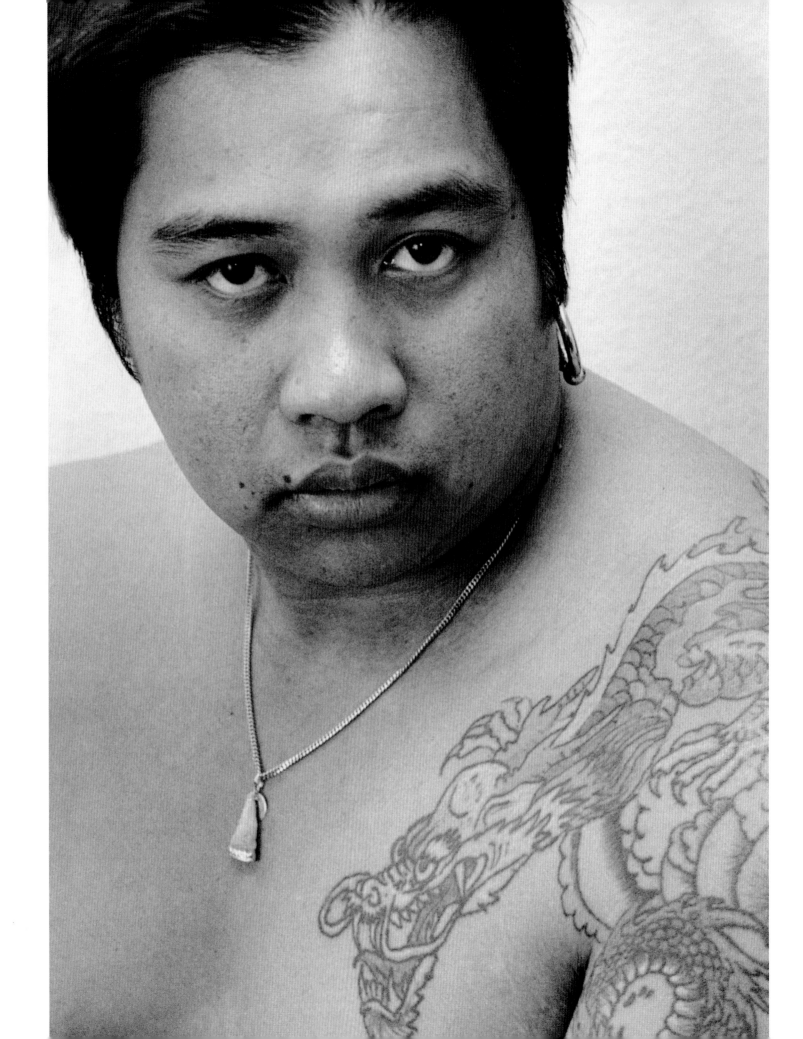

On September 28, 1974, three year-old Tuy Buckner was flown to America from Allambie orphanage in Saigon, Vietnam. Although he was taken to a place that was worlds away from the war, bombings, and systematic sweeps through the villages of the Mekong Delta, Tuy remained terrified to go outside his adoptive parents' home.

"I can't put words to those early memories," he says. "They come in dreams, in nightmares. Without my adoptive parents' love and support, I'm not sure where I would be." Tuy was adopted into a large family in Berkeley, California with six brothers and sisters. His parents adopted five children from India, Vietnam, and the United States. Tuy's family held meetings every week. Topics varied, but adoption was frequently the center of discussion. "My mother spoke from her heart, and was always honest. My strength comes from her. She prepared us by saying, 'If you ever do meet your birth parents, they may be totally different from what you expect.'

"As a child, I often thought about locating my birth family. If I could find them, I thought I would write a letter. We'd start corresponding, then we'd plan a rendezvous by a river. The sun would be setting. Little lotus flowers and cherry blossoms would surround us. I guess I must have had a child's expectations, because the real meeting was like nothing I'd have expected in a million years." Tuy's adoptive mother, an attorney, with specialties in public health and Asian studies, had been active in the Peace Movement during the Vietnam War. Knowing that Tuy had always wanted to return to Vietnam, she arranged for him to participate in a Peace Walk there in 1991, aimed at ending the U.S. trade embargo.

"I was twenty," he remembers. "Since my mother and I had traveled together a lot, it seemed like just another trip at first. But it turned out to be a very emotional experience. The reality of landing in Hanoi was rough. I closed up and cried a bit. I was American. I didn't know Vietnamese culture. It wasn't a part of me. The peace walk went from Hanoi to Saigon, stopping in villages and cities, schools and hospitals along the way. I saw the poverty of the Vietnamese people. Even though vegetation hid most of the remnants of the war, you could see tanks, and whole mine fields were fenced off because they were so dangerous. Still, people went into the mine fields to retrieve scrap metal to sell. Thirty year-old mines killed water buffaloes and blew off the limbs of farmers."

Initially, Tuy and his mother had planned to visit Tuy's first orphanage in the Mekong Delta, but they were unable to get government permission for the trip, so they went to Cambodia instead. In Phnom Penh, Tuy met many young people his own

Tuy, age three, in an orphanage in Vietnam, 1974

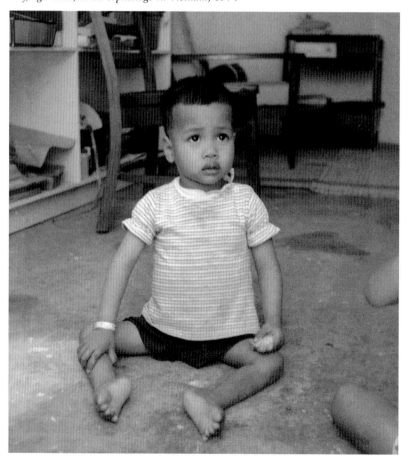

age who still lived in orphanages. He spent time with them, understanding their lives, and the life he would likely have had if he had not come to America.

Two years later, Tuy and a friend, David, returned to Vietnam for the wedding of Vietnamese friends from Berkeley. They stayed for three months—enough time to search. "From my birth certificate, I knew I needed to go to Sadec on the Mekong River, so we rented a car with a driver. But the bridge to Sadec was washed out by floods. In Can Tho, the next larger town, we found the nun, Nguyen Thi Tot, who had been in the Sadec orphanage at the time I was there; she was the woman who had signed my birth documents. She told me that many adoptees came to search for their parents. 'Finding family may be impossible,' she said, then added, 'But you can write to me as if I am your mother.'

"David and I went back to Sadec again after attending the wedding in Danang. The bridge was passable by then. I wanted to see the region where I came from, and I'd heard they had great duck. I didn't have any false expectations. I knew it was unlikely I would find my family. We planned to spend an hour or two at the Sadec orphanage where I'd stayed, and then eat some duck and leave. After that, I didn't plan to return again.

"When David and I sat down with the nuns on this second trip to the Delta, they said, 'Yes, we remember you.' They were polite. It was the appropriate thing to say. I'm sure they didn't really know me, but it was comforting to have a connection there. As we spoke, a large crowd gathered outside to peek through the church windows, wanting to see the American Vietnamese.

"We were told that many of the records from that time had been destroyed, but one of the nuns showed me a book of records from the early seventies. I already had a picture of myself as a child, and I knew my Vietnamese name from my birth certificate: Nguyen Quoc Tuy, 'Man of Nguyen Dynasty.' I found my entry, with my picture, my name, and the date I arrived in 1971. But no family name. The experience was like an emotional roller coaster; every elation was followed by a crushing disappointment. Yes, here is your entry. No, there is no family name. I had come to another dead end."

Tuy and David made a donation to the orphanage as a token of their gratitude, and the nuns arranged for an elaborate meal of the famous duck for everyone to enjoy. "While the food was being prepared, a woman named Phien dropped by for her monthly visit to the nuns. 'Phien was here at the orphanage with you,' the nuns told me. They showed her my page in the record book. She looked at my picture, then back up at me, and then just stared at me in recognition. 'I took care of this baby when I was a teenager. I know your mother! I was just going to visit some of your relatives.' To think Phien had chosen that day, that hour, that moment to drop by. . ."

After going by motor scooter out to the village, a two hour round trip, Phien returned with Tuy's mother, Nguyen Thi Be. "I remember seeing her for the first time," Tuy says. "She had a puzzled look on her face. The nuns were pushing her toward me and saying, 'Your son!' My hair was long, in a ponytail. My mother grabbed my head and started separating the hair on my scalp. When she found a scar she recognized, she said, 'This is my son!' At that point, I went numb."

Tuy wanted to do something special for his mother, and arranged for her to return with him to Saigon for the three days before his return trip to America. "She was so excited, she couldn't sleep. She didn't know I had become disabled with polio in the orphanage, that I needed crutches and braces. She inspected my legs and the scars. She was very sad about my legs. She combed my hair. Her English was minimal, so we communicated more with looks and actions rather than with words. Though I was greatly loved in my adoptive family, I never experienced this kind of emotion before. It was unexpected. It was more than I could handle."

To Tuy, the story of his birth parents' relationship is like the fairy tale of Rapunzel, only in reverse. His father, Pantaleon

Mance, was from the Philippines. Because he had an expertise in communication, he had come to Vietnam with an engineering crew to help the South Vietnamese war effort. "His job was to receive radio transmissions before they were censored. He worked in a tower that was guarded by military police, and wasn't allowed to come down for long periods of time because the transmissions were classified. My mother would visit him with food to eat or baskets of laundry. She would yell up to the window, he would lower a basket, and then he'd pull it back up, full of food and clean clothes. Obviously, at some time my father must have come down from the tower! But he left Vietnam without ever knowing that Nguyen Thi Be was pregnant with his son.

"After she had me, my mother became ill. She knew the orphanage would feed me, and that I would be cared for by the nuns. When she came back a few years later, she was told I had gone to America. The way she dealt with it was to say to herself and the family that I was dead. She placed a baby picture of me on her mantle. According to Vietnamese tradition,

I was already an ancestor."

Tuy wanted to commemorate their reunion by giving his mother something special. He pulled his hair back in a long braid and had it cut off. "I wrapped an eye-of-the-dragon pendant around the braid and gave it to my mother. I told her, 'This is a gift to mark our past, to mark the time we never had. It should not be token of sadness, but a token of happiness, because we have our whole future ahead of us now.'"

When Tuy returned home from that trip, "it was like my life in America meant nothing," he recalls. "Before, I had been plugging along, glad to be an 'all-American Asian guy.' Now I questioned everything. I couldn't go back to school. I ended up hiding in my room. I failed all my classes. Everything for the next six months was a blur. Before, Vietnam was just a word. Now, I was the oldest son. I had six more brothers and sisters living in a village near Sadec. I knew my Vietnamese family lived in poverty. Again, it was more than I could handle."

Since then, Tuy has been back to Vietnam many times. In 1995, he bought a house there and deeded it to his Vietnamese family, so if anything happens to him, they will be provided for. He contributes to his siblings' education and job training. In addition, he has found a more personal way to honor them.

"I wanted to create something permanent to symbolize finding my mother and father," he says. "I have a tattoo of a water dragon on my arm that represents me traveling over the ocean and back again. My mother is represented by the phoenix. When I met her for the first time, it was like rising from the ashes of war. For all intents and purposes, I was dead to her and she was dead to me. Yet we survived. A larger dragon represents my birth father and the burden of being a man. The permanence of tattoos expresses the fact that there is no changing the truth—they are my biological parents."

Tuy has a deep appreciation for his American parents. "My dream was to introduce my two mothers. When I was staying in Vietnam a few years ago, I invited my American mother, Kris Seeman, to visit me. I brought my Vietnamese mother with me to the airport to pick her up. She held flowers for my American mother. I knew enough of the language to translate. My Vietnamese mother said, 'I thank you very much for taking care of my son during those years I could not. Thank you for raising him in the correct way.' She understands what it takes to raise a child. My adoptive mother hugged her and said, 'Thank you for the opportunity to raise your son.' Since then, my moms have spent a lot of time together. They both respect and like each other. I love them both. They know they are both my mothers."

FOLLOWING THE BIRTH OF THEIR FIRST CHILD, ALICIN, THE REIDYS DECIDED to complete their family by adopting a three year-old girl, Nicki, through Social Services. Two children sounded just right to them.

"Then, out of the blue, Social Services contacted us about adopting John, who was the youngest of three siblings," Cheryl explains. "Although we felt our family was complete, we were inexplicably drawn to this idea. After thinking it over for days, we called the agency back and said, 'It's either all of them or none of them!' Because if children have been separated from their mother, you can't separate them from each other."

She and Bill made a commitment to the children before they even walked through the door of the foster home. They couldn't disappoint all three by changing their minds after seeing them. "I was appalled at the setting and circumstances of the foster home," Cheryl remembers. "Donna was in a dress that didn't fit her very well and her hair was all over the place. John was skinny, pale, and sick," Bill recalls. "When Alissa came in from school, it was obvious she was the big kid on the block, in charge of everything. She was very quiet, always watching, always checking things out. She had an 'evil eye' that could freeze water."

Alissa, now twenty-three says, "I was very quiet, but I was also pretty angry."

"You were saying a lot, without saying a word," Bill comments.

Cheryl adds, "You ruled the roost."

"She had been a little mother to John and Donna. She took responsibility and tried to

From Left: Leah, Alissa, Cheryl, Bill and John

take care of them," Bill explains.

"All I wanted was to go back to my mom," says Alissa. Because she had been trying to hold her family together, she would not allow Cheryl and Bill to parent her or her siblings. "It took more than six months for her call me anything—even bitch. I told her over and over, 'Call me anything. Call me Cheryl, you don't have to call me mom.' But I was a non-person to her for a long time. She was suspicious of everything we did and very protective of John and Donna."

They also had many more rules than Alissa was used to. "No, you can't get up at six in the morning and run out in the street, for instance." Cheryl says. "Yes, we do eat breakfast. And, yes, I do comb your hair before you go to school."

Social Services did not inform the Reidys that the children had previously lived in several foster homes. "Naturally, this instability deeply impacted them," Cheryl explains. "If adoption is about parenting, Social Services needs to give parents a shot. They need to provide the full, true story about what their children have been through. Otherwise, the system is tying our hands. We had to work hard to piece together their story."

Alissa remembers overhearing her mother, Beatrice, explain to Alissa's biological father, Sam, why she was letting the children be adopted. "Sam was upset, but Beatrice felt she was doing the best thing for us by giving us up. She wanted to be in our lives, but she didn't plan on actually getting us back."

Beatrice had been abused as a child and was out on the streets at a very young age. Her boyfriend Sam was much older. "She was fourteen when she had me," Alissa explains. "She tried to take care of us, but she got into drugs and alcohol, so it was hard. I don't have any good memories. I remember incidents, mostly with John and Donna, where we saw bad things happen. Really bad situations."

Alissa has blanked out the memory of actually being taken from Beatrice. "I don't remember feeling devastated, although I must have been," she reflects. "I can't remember whether I thought I would be with the Reidys for a long time, or whether I was afraid I wouldn't be. It took a long time for me to accept them as my parents."

Cheryl remembers that Alissa seemed devastated. "She became quiet, inward, and needed to be in control at all times. John had an easier time connecting with us. It did take him a long time to begin talking, though. Social Services thought he was hearing impaired. But he wasn't."

"He took everything in," Bill recalls. "He didn't say anything, but he took it all in."

"It threw me when Donna was so solicitous," Cheryl adds. "But that wasn't real, either. Neither Alissa nor Donna could really be themselves with us. One was searching to fit, and the other was searching for her mom to come back. John could be real with us. He did not walk well for a long time, so we ended up holding him a lot. The third week the children were in our home, they all got the chicken pox. Bill and I were up pacing the floor with John, because he couldn't sleep from all the discomfort. John doesn't remember anything about his life before coming to us. But his playing was violent and angry. He struggles with anger to this day."

Beatrice did not know where her children had been placed, but she prayed that God would protect them, and hoped they were in the same adoptive home together. She found herself searching faces on the street, hoping to see them.

"I was five years old when they took me away," Alissa says. "I didn't see Beatrice again until I was fifteen." Alissa was working at McDonald's, her first job, when Beatrice stepped up to the counter to order. "She looked at me and said, 'Oh, I've been waiting so long. Don't you recognize me? I thought, out of all my kids, you would recognize me.' But I didn't recognize her. The picture in my mind was totally different from how she actually looked. She freaked me out. I left her standing there and ran downstairs. I was crying. Someone took me home and I told my parents what happened."

Alissa and Donna were already having a very difficult time in school and at home. After seeing Beatrice, the problems escalated. Alissa began running away to New York City, took the subway to Harlem, and lived on the streets. When she occasionally returned home, Bill and Cheryl had no idea what to do with her.

Eventually, Alissa was hospitalized for bulimia and turned sixteen in the hospital. Beatrice learned that Alissa was having problems and dropped by the high school looking for her daughters. She stopped a couple of students in the hall and asked if they knew a mulatto girl by the name of Alissa. The students gave Beatrice the Reidys' last name. Word passed through the hallways that Alissa and Donna's 'real' mother was looking for them. The sisters searched the school for Beatrice instead of going to classes.

"The school never notified us," Cheryl says. "Beatrice called me from the pay phone. I could hear the principal screaming in the background, 'Get out of here or I am going to call the police!' She didn't even know my first name. She was desperate to know if Alissa was all right, because she had heard that she had been in the hospital. I said to her, 'Look, if you need to know your kids, this isn't the way to go about it.

Let's sit down and talk about it.'"

Cheryl and Beatrice met at McDonald's, while Alissa was still in school, and talked for five hours. "I looked into Beatrice's eyes and saw my Alissa's beautiful eyes. We agreed that if she wanted to get to know the kids, it would have to be done slowly, over time, with some predictability. Alissa, Donna, and John would need some control as well.

"When the kids got home from school, they acted like nothing happened. Finally I said I knew Beatrice had been at school that day."

Alissa, Donna, and John still struggle with their relationship with Beatrice, but they have come a long way. Knowing they can pick up the phone and speak with her is a relief to them. They have all worked hard to be a family. Cheryl admires Beatrice. "She's a strong person, a survivor with a great deal of dignity. She found a way to finally not be crazy within a crazy family. She gave her children a chance to be raised in a stable, loving family, and I have a great deal of respect for her. Alissa, Donna, and John needed a stable home to become who they've become today.

"But they also needed to know Beatrice, and to know Beatrice would be all right, too."

KATHRYN SHELLEY

ALL HER LIFE, TEXAS ARTIST KATHRYN SHELLEY FELT DRAWN TO SEEK ANSWERS
to philosophical and spiritual questions. "It now strikes me that, as curious as I've been,
the one line of questioning I never pursued was probing my own reality as an adopted
child," she reflects. "I seldom allowed myself to think in any conscious way that I had
another mother out there. Whenever I tried, it was like grabbing smoke—there was nothing to hold onto. Although I can't remember an age when I didn't know I was adopted,
the meaning of adoption took shape over time, through the absence of words. My only
fantasy was that my mother was a hobo riding trains, and that she was destitute. I could
not connect to the concept of another mother, and the existence of another father and
extended family never entered my mind."

It was not until 1983, when Kathryn was twenty-one and a college student, that she
felt compelled to know more about herself. "My adoptive mother had a two-page letter
of background information about my birth mother, and I stole it. Then I contacted
Sante Fe, where my records were housed. Because I was feeling ambivalent and guilty, I
was hesitant to make the phone call. A clerk answered the phone and when I requested
my information, she said, 'Those records are absolutely closed to you.' I hung up and
thought, 'You should feel guilty and hesitant—you're treading in places you are not meant
to tread.'"

A few years later, Kathryn had minor surgery that required more medical information
than she had access to, and her search for her birth family intensified. "Here I was, an

adult facing an adult situation—releasing liability should anything happen to me during surgery—and I couldn't even provide the simplest medical history."

Within the year, she attended her first ALMA (Adoptees' Liberty Movement Association) meeting. "I sat in the meeting, very calm and composed, thinking that searching was an idea I could take or leave. I listened to an older man speak gently about his need to see 'his' face. He was giving words to emotions that I could barely allow myself to have. A birth mother was at the meeting with her newly found son. They looked like two peas in a pod: same body type, same gestures, same use of language. I looked at them and thought, 'Oh, my God. I could really have someone I resonate with out there.' Afterwards, walking to my car, I started sobbing, and cried all the way home. Emotions were gurgling up from somewhere. That was the beginning."

Kathryn decided to fly to her adoptive parents' respective homes to end the secrecy about her need to find her birth mother. Her father still lived in the town in New Mexico where she had grown up. "When I told him I needed to find my birth mother, his position was, 'I think it makes a lot of sense that you want to know more information. But keep in mind she's moved on with her life, and you could be interrupting things.'" At that time, Geraldine Ferraro was running for vice president, and her father added, "Imagine what it would be like for someone like Geraldine Ferraro if some child from her past surfaced and wrecked everything."

In spite of his reservations, Kathryn's father took her to the county clerk he had known for years to find out what records might be available. "The clerk asked what my interests were, and I felt caught between what I wanted to say and the fact that my dad was sitting right there. I said something about being curious and having my parents' support. Though I was twenty-six, it still seemed important that she knew my parents approved.

"The woman made a phone call and, in minutes, a copy of my records were in her hands. I leaned over her shoulder as she opened the envelope and pulled out a copy of my relinquishment papers with my original name and my birth mother's name on it. As she read the information out loud, matter-of-factly, she glanced up at me and realized tears were streaming down my face. I had no idea I had been given a birth name: Shelley Christine Cain. I had never considered the possibility. And my other mother was suddenly a real person with a real name: Janice Irene Cain."

Despite an ominous notice which read "NOT TO BE OPENED UNLESS BY WRITTEN ORDER OF THE COURT," the clerk gave Kathryn her records. Afterwards, she and her father drove the twenty minutes to his home without discussing what had just happened. They had never figured out how to bridge such silences between them, or how to discuss a topic of that magnitude. "All I wanted to do on the drive home was curl up with that document and just breathe it in," she recalls. "But I set it aside.

"That night I was so tired and drained and emotional. I went to bed and was finally alone with my papers. Over and over, I wrote my original name and Jan's name. During the next weeks, I spent a lot of time writing those names. It was my way of realizing I had really existed before I was six months old."

At the bottom of the relinquishment papers, another woman's signature was next to Kathryn's birth mother's. "I immediately spun fantasies about who this person was to my mother," Kathryn recalls. "Was she her dearest, best friend?" The papers indicated that the woman was from Colorado. After more research, Kathryn found her and learned she was retired, but that she had been a social worker at the Florence Crittenton Home, a refuge for unwed mothers back in the 1960s. "I asked her what the situation was like then, if women got to see their children, if they got to hold them, how they said goodbye, or if they did. What she disclosed was troubling. Young women often entered the home under assumed names.

Wearing Jan's necklace, Kathryn stands before her own self-portrait

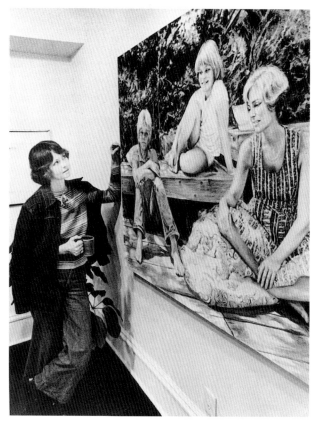

Janice Cain looking at her painting, circa 1970s

It was their choice about whether or not to see their babies, but they were encouraged not to. At Florence Crittenton, there were about forty births a week. "Due to the sheer volume of babies being placed for adoption, Colorado worked out deals with other states, which is how I came to be placed in New Mexico," explains Kathryn. She was able to obtain a copy of Jan's birth certificate, which revealed that her family was from Minneapolis. Jan's father's name was Joseph Dale Cain. Kathryn called all the Joseph Cains she could locate, using the excuse that she was on a high school reunion committee, tracking down the current names and addresses of alumni. "I ended up with one directory left, from White Bear Lake. Just one Joseph Cain left to call in the Minneapolis area. I couldn't bring myself to make the call, and asked my dearest friend to do it for me.

"I was upstairs, she was downstairs, and I heard her ask, 'So what happened?' When she finally came up the stairs, she was crying. She said, 'I think we've found your family. Your grandmother said she was really surprised I didn't know that they lost Jan five years ago due to diabetic complications.' I would later realize that her death in 1983 was the same year in college that I felt an urge to find her.

"I couldn't comprehend the reality that I'd found my family, and that the person I needed to know once again was gone. I felt distant and numb."

Kathryn struggled that afternoon between a fear of being rejected by her grandparents and her sense that they were the only people who could understand her grief. "When I decided to call them, I wrote out my name, phone number, address, and the first sentence of what I wanted to say. I thought it was entirely possible that I might forget my own name," she remembers. "An older woman answered the phone. In my raw, shaky voice I asked, 'Do you have a minute to talk?' She replied, 'Well, yes. Are you in some kind of trouble?' And I said, 'No, but does the name of the Florence Crittenton Home mean anything to you?'

"'No,' she replied.

"'Well, I know that Janice Cain was your daughter, and I think she was my mother.' There was a long silence. Then she burst into tears and said, 'Oh, honey, I hope so.' After we'd talked a while, she asked, 'Do you want to talk to your grandfather?' Then she yelled to him, 'Dale, it's Jan's baby! Jan's baby is on the phone.'

"My grandfather got on the phone and excitedly said, 'Can this be true?'" Kathryn's grandmother ran outside, where people who had come to pick her up were waiting in the driveway, and told them about Kathryn's call. "My Aunt Verna, who was in the car, bolted into the house and got on the phone. That was an amazing moment. I heard my own voice on the other end. I was so taken aback by that sound—my first real proof that this was my family.

"In that first conversation, my grandparents told me that my birth father, Skip, lived around the bend of the lake from them. They wanted to call him for me. Although he lived within walking distance, they had barely spoken during the twenty-six years since my birth. I said to myself, 'There's a father? Around the bend?'

"By the fourth time we talked, I gave in to my grandfather's continued requests to contact Skip. The next morning, I got a phone call, and there was this man's voice saying, 'Kathryn, this is your father.' When I spoke, he said, 'Your voice sounds just like Jan's. I feel like I've stepped into a time warp.'" Kathryn recalls, "He had just told his wife about me thirty minutes before. She got on the phone and said, 'If only I'd known about you, I would have tried to find you myself. You are Skip's only biological child.' I couldn't believe the grace of this woman, or my good fortune."

Spectacular clouds filled the sky the day Kathryn finally flew to meet her birth families. Her grandparents, her birth mother's two sisters, her birth father, and his wife all came to greet her. There was a connection between the families other than Kathryn. Verna, Jan's younger sister, had also relinquished a child, eight months before Jan. Skip knew her secret. So Kathryn's Aunt Verna, and Kathryn's father, Skip, were together for the first time in years, waiting at the airport to reunite with Jan's daughter.

Kathryn remembers, "As I walked off the plane, I saw them all standing together waiting for me. It was like an out-of-body experience. I remember watching myself walking toward them. All sensations felt magnified. The first person to run up to me was my grandmother. She scooped me up, then pulled back to look at me, grabbed my hands, and said, 'You have Jan's hands.'

"Then my Aunt Barb, Jan's older sister, embraced me and said, 'I love you.' I wanted to sink into the emotions, yet I didn't even know her last name and she was saying she loved me.

"Skip's hug was so full and embracing. I felt my heart opening. And then I saw my grandfather's aged face and

take me further. I had to sit down right there. It was as if my art was on their wall. I felt so connected to Jan, and yet she wasn't there. How could I embrace such a connection, make it real, and let go and grieve all at the same time?"

Her Aunt Barb took Kathryn by the hand and led her to a photograph of her mother. "This was the first time I saw her face. I traced her features with my fingers as I wept, and then gradually became aware that everyone was still standing quietly behind me. I put the picture down. My grandfather brought out champagne and everyone made a lovely toast to welcome me."

Later, Kathryn started down the stairs to the lower level of their home. "Again, I had the recognition that I'd been there before," she says. "I knew those stairs. I knew which way to turn to find my mother's old bedroom. Jan's paintings and drawings were everywhere. I was surrounded by everything I knew."

"WE SLEPT IN JAN'S BED TOGETHER. I CURLED UP WITH MY HEAD ON HER CHEST, SINKING INTO THE RECOGNITION THAT THIS RHYTHM, THIS HEARTBEAT, THIS BREATHING PATTERN, THIS SMELL WAS SO FAMILIAR."

---

thought, 'Oh, I resemble you.' My Aunt Verna was the last one to come up to me."

On the ride to her grandparents' home, Kathryn stared at Skip, mesmerized by the concept that this was her father. "I really wanted to touch him," she recalls. "I will never know how to explain it, but when we turned down the street to Jan's home by this beautiful lake, everything was so familiar to me. Before Skip pointed it out, I knew. 'That's the house.' As we stood on the front deck overlooking the lake, he was as white as a ghost. He said, 'Jan would have loved this so much, and really needed it.' A part of me was just screaming inside. I felt so split by this experience."

The rest of the family began arriving. "They led me to the front door, and I walked in with everyone behind me," Kathryn remembers. "As I entered, the first thing I saw were Jan's portrait paintings on the walls. My legs felt weak and would not

The next day, she and Skip took a canoe from his brother's cabin and headed down to the water. "The only request I had made of Skip prior to meeting him was to spend time with him on the water. It felt symbolic that I should learn my story there. He talked candidly, which I deeply appreciated," Kathryn says. "He said what I imagine was hard for him to say—that he didn't make a decision, and that by not doing so, a decision was made. Even though he and Jan were engaged, he listened to his family, worried about their position in society, and succumbed to pressures and influences. He suppressed any thoughts about me. That was not my fantasy. But it was truth I was looking for. I needed to know if Jan had held me. Skip didn't know. Now I will never know if my mother held me in her arms."

The third day of Kathryn's stay, Verna came to spend the night. "She was my closest connection to Jan," Kathryn says.

"She was her kindred sister, a birth mother, and an artist as well. We slept in Jan's bed together. I curled up with my head on her chest, sinking into the recognition that this rhythm, this heartbeat, this breathing pattern, this smell was so familiar. It was the most comforting place. We stayed awake most of the night as she told me stories about my mother. Listening to her breathe was deeply moving, and awakened a hunger for what I had missed."

The next eighteen months were filled with feeding that hunger. "I was a sponge soaking in every detail and I needed to be with them as much as I could. I needed to watch them drink milk. I needed to watch them walk across the room. When I'd return to my home in Texas, I'd fall apart."

Kathryn felt she had to be steeped in knowledge of Jan's life before she could begin accepting her death. She wanted to be surrounded by Jan's artwork, to 'try her on'. "I needed to understand what was inherent in me—my talent, the things I was drawn to, the spiritual way I move through life. I tried on every clue they gave me about my mother, whether it fit me or not. I listened to stories about how she took in the homeless, and I took in the homeless. I bought hats, because she wore hats. I wore her clothes and jewelry. The first Christmas, my grandparents sent me Jan's afghan. When I pulled it out of the box, I wanted to smell her in the wool, but it had been cleaned. I wrapped myself in it and rocked and rocked. It was so bittersweet."

Over the next five years, Kathryn courageously thought through her life's complexities. "My usual method of coping— being sweet and kind and accepting—wasn't cutting it any-

more. I realized that all my life, the secrecy of who my relatives were, and the required silencing of my mother's experience and my own, were forces that disavowed our connection to each other. I felt my identity being shaken up and reordered in a way that was finally honest."

In 1995, Kathryn had an art show in St. Augustine, Florida, a town of cobblestone streets and horse-drawn carriages, where her mother had lived. The show was titled 'Claiming Connections: The Art of Kathryn Shelley and Jan Cain.' The most striking aspect of the show was not the similarities in their work, but the artists' ability to capture the essence of the people in their portraits. "I know I would have been a painter no matter what," Kathryn feels. "But had I grown up with Jan, I imagine I'd have altered the way I paint in order to not be like her. Because I wasn't raised with her, my talent emerged in its purest form—and it's very much like Jan's."

The show opened the weekend of Kathryn's birthday. "There was media attention, so people who had known Jan attended the reception," she recalls. "They were generous in sharing their stories about her with me. They saw much of Jan in me, but without the vested interest her family naturally had. I was beginning to feel more detached and separate from her. She moved from being the fantasy mother I was either under-attached or over-attached to, into a place of balance. Though it was a profoundly intimate show, I was there representing myself. I had finally moved from needing to get inside Jan's body—that primal, creaturely, instinct stuff—to claiming my own. Now I find myself identifying with a quote from Alice Walker: 'In search of my mother's garden, I found my own.'"

JACK RYAN

On June 20, 1985, Brett and Kip Schaefer traveled with their mother, Carol, down the coast road from San Francisco to Mission Viejo to meet their nineteen year-old brother, Jack Ryan, for the first time. Neither boy had known that their mother had another son until a year earlier, when Carol had begun searching for him.

As Brett and Kip anticipated gaining an older brother, Mark and David Rehnberg, the brothers Jack grew up with, feared losing him to the strangers who were his other family. Mark, aged nine, and David, who was eight, are the biological sons of Jack's adoptive mother, Rosemary Rehnberg.

Fifteen years after they first met, all five young men gathered at a friend's apartment in Manhattan to discuss the impact that the 1985 reunion had on all of their lives.

Both Brett and Kip remember being completely shocked when their mother, Carol, told them she had given up a son for adoption. "There were no clues," recalls Brett, who was thirteen at the time.

"I think she was acting funny right around the time she told us," remembers Kip, who was then eleven. "We were fairly young, so we didn't understand what it all meant. My initial reaction was positive. I thought it was going to be a new experience—positive and unique. I was totally open to it. I never once feared anything negative; I never thought he might be a psychopath or anything like that."

Kip's opinion about his mother didn't change after he'd heard her news. "My parents were divorced, and Mom had dated other people, so it wasn't unusual for me to think

n left: Kip, Brett, Jack, Mark, and David

that she'd been with someone before my father."

For Brett, however, it was strange to think that his mother was like the people on talk shows who discussed having had children at a young age. "It was a big thing to learn that I had a brother. But finding out Mom had sex when she was very young wasn't a huge deal. It didn't change the way I viewed her. Kip kidded with me that I wasn't the oldest anymore. But I was older than him, and that was all that mattered at the time."

"Brett and I were very competitive," Kip recalls. "He always had to have the upper hand. So the fact that there was someone older than Brett, who would have the upper hand on him—I know I threw that up in his face at some point."

Both speculated about who their brother might be. "John Elway had just been drafted by the Broncos, and was also being wooed by the major leagues. He went to Stanford University, so we wondered if our brother could be John Elway," Brett recalls.

show my buddies. His date was fine! When we learned he was a water polo player and had been in the Junior Olympics, I thought, 'Okay, now he feels more like one of us.'"

Kip remembers his mom's first conversation with Jack's adoptive mother, Rosemary. "Mom was so excited to learn that Jack had been raised by a really special woman. And she was thrilled that everything had worked out. She had a sense of relief after talking with Jack's mother. That was nice."

"My mom likes to talk," Jack explains. "So she probably told my whole life story right there. Carol's call was not totally out of the blue. I had received non-identifying information from Catholic Social Services. It took me a long time to get back to her. It was a lot to take in at that time in my life. I was graduating high school. That summer I was on the junior national team for water polo. We traveled to Hawaii and to China, where we played against their Olympic team. Truthfully, though I was in her heart and mind for nineteen

---

"I LOOKED AT JACK AND SAID, 'YOU'RE ADOPTED?' AND HE SAID, 'YEAH.' IN A WAY, I FELT LIKE IT TAINTED THE RELATIONSHIP, LIKE IT WASN'T

"During the year our mother searched for him, she began spending more energy away from us than we were accustomed to," says Kip. "Her focus was on finding Jack. It was just a difference, neither positive nor negative. I knew she was going through a hard time and needed our support. She still went to all our ball games and took care of us. My mom always has all sorts of things going on, but she started to be more forgetful about the day-to-day things. Making lunch, getting us to school, and picking us up seemed less ritualized, and we were more independent. Her emotions were flying around. We had to get used to sharing her attention."

Brett doesn't remember being affected that way. "To be honest, at thirteen you're pretty focused on yourself. Both of us were involved in sports and afternoon activities. It was definitely a cool experience. I remember when we received our first photographs of Jack. I took one from his senior prom to

years, I felt like I already had a family. At times, while growing up, I was curious about who these other people might be. When she contacted me, I felt blank at first. I think I decided not to feel anything. Now I realize I tortured her terribly by not responding right away."

"The waiting probably did torture her a little," Brett comments.

"I always knew I was adopted," Jack adds. "I grew up praying at bedtime for her well-being."

David, Jack's youngest brother, says he always knew Jack was adopted, but Mark did not recall ever being told. "For me, it was a shock," he admits. "I just thought he was our brother. I remember the exact moment when they told me. My mom was washing her hair in the bathroom and Jack was standing right by her. Something came up, I can't remember what. And I looked at Jack and said, 'You're adopted?' And he said, 'Yeah.'

In a way, I felt like it tainted the relationship, like it wasn't real. It 'illegitimized' it for me. My family acted nonchalant, like it wasn't a big deal. No one talked about it. To me, this was big news. I thought about it a lot."

"That's pretty heavy," Jack says. "I thought you knew. I consider all of you just the innocent bystanders—the ones being affected by Carol's and my interest in knowing each other."

"We were young," David says. "I was more interested in G.I. Joe than in understanding the whole thing. And Jack wasn't all distraught about it. Seeing no change in him made it easier."

David adds, "It's not like you were going to sit down with your eight year-old brother and say, 'You know, I'm feeling really upset.'"

"It must have been hard, though," Kip comments. "You were in a whirlwind: 'Okay, so Jack's adopted.' Then all of a sudden, Jack's birth mother and brothers are on their way to meet you. Two brothers—that must have been strange."

"It really got to me," Mark says. "I wondered if she was going to take him away and we would never see him again."

The car ride down to Mission Viejo, Brett recalls, was miserable. "The coast road took a long time. I built a tent, like a little fort, in the back seat. And when we drove up to their house, I was the last one out of the car."

"I was at the window looking for them, probably pacing," Jack recalls. "Mark and David were playing in the backyard. I went outside, and Mom said, 'Wait, wait! You're going out? There was a hill that came down towards our house, and I could see their car coming over the hill. The driver was looking for a house. So the first meeting was just us, because I happened to walk outside right then. It was pretty surreal. Kip got out of the car and came running up first."

Kip says, "I remember walking up to you and saying, 'I'm Kip.' You said, 'Well, I know.'"

"Then Carol walked around the car toward me," adds Jack. "Carol projects warmth. I caught that right off the bat."

"It was odd to see my mom embracing her long-lost son,"

says Kip. "Just to see that kind of emotion toward someone she hadn't known. In that initial hug, there was a lot of pent-up emotion in her body."

"I remember it being a real nice, comfortable hug," Jack says. "But truthfully, I was worrying about everyone's feelings and wondering, 'Is Mom coming outside?' I worried about my mom's feelings throughout. She had told me she was curious and excited to meet Carol. She may have been acting that way for my benefit. From the time she came outside, I tried to make sure that neither of their feelings would get hurt. I tried to do that for too long, by not letting anyone know how I felt."

"Do you still worry about everyone's feelings?" Kip asked him.

"Now I figure everyone has to be able to deal with how it is for them. But I did worry about it for a long time. It took me until I was thirty."

"I was worried about his mom," Brett says.

"I thought, do we have a right to come barging into his adoptive family?" Kip adds.

"I think our situation worked out very well," Brett continues, "but I don't think every situation works out that way. I'm not totally sold on the search thing, because I can't base everything on our experience. I think it's very hard on the adoptive parents. It's a big intrusion on their lives. There may be insecurity, stuff like that."

"So you thought about everyone's feelings, too?" Jack asks him. Brett nods.

"That's how I felt," says Mark. "Here comes his birth mom. Is she going to take him away from us? We had to wait to see what would happen. Is he going to be with them for Christmas and holidays, instead of with us?"

"My mom was interested in meeting them," Jack says. "But truthfully, she thought we would meet and that would pretty much be the end of it—she'd go on with her life. I don't think there is any way to do that. Once you open the door, you may as well try to work together."

"I was talking to Mom recently," Mark says. "She said the exact same thing. She expected to just meet once. When Carol said, 'I want to have a relationship', my mom said, 'what?'"

"If she had it her way," says Kip, "Jack would be there for Christmas and all the holidays. And I can see why his mom and dad would feel, 'Hey, we raised this kid. This is our family too.' I always felt like I didn't want that added pressure of thinking about the adoptive family, because I wanted to get close to Jack and be his brother. There was a natural bond, but I always felt tentative because I knew it wasn't necessarily our place. They needed to be the ones to open the door—it shouldn't be us slamming through the door."

Brett adds, "I also think if I were in Jack's shoes and my birth mother found me and said afterwards, 'Okay, it was nice meeting you,' and he never heard from her again."

". . . That would be bad," concludes Jack.

"There is no perfect solution," Kip reflects. "I didn't know how Jack felt about us. I always sensed there was some feeling, but also some hesitation, so I kind of put the brakes on. You just have to get on with it and see what happens. We've gotten closer over the years—it just takes time. The four of us, Jack's four brothers, don't know each other well, but I don't think we would have any problem getting along."

"You two were not born until I was ten, later than I had hoped," Jack says, looking at Mark and David. "But it was the beginning of a lifelong relationship, for you have shared my life and my memories. We share parents and relatives whom we love. Naturally, we have become friends. At the age of nineteen, I began a lifelong relationship with Brett and Kip, brothers who entered my life later than I had hoped. You two have shared my life and memories, and have become my friends. We also share a parent and relatives whom we love. It is a privilege and an honor to be your brother."

LITTLE SCRAPS OF PAPER BESIDE THE PHONE HELD SHREDS OF INFORMATION about the strangers who were soon to become family. David Stitzhal didn't want to forget to tell his partner Laurel anything the adoption agency had said when she got home.

A nineteen year-old birth mother named Megan had chosen them to be the parents for her child, who was due in three weeks. Megan and her boyfriend Andy were high school sweethearts, struggling in their five-year relationship. She didn't want Andy to marry her just because she was pregnant, and she didn't want her mother to have to take care of the child. As for the information David had just been given, it included the fact that she and Andy both loved the outdoors. Andy played Hackeysack and liked to construct computers. Megan loved music, especially the Grateful Dead. "It was a strange collection of facts about two human beings," David, an environmentalist specializing in recycling, recalls. "We had been 'chosen.'"

Based on minimal descriptions provided by the counselor, Laurel and David had to decide if they were willing to take the next step. They sifted through the information about Megan and Andy. In the process, they called the adoption counselor several times. "We were in this odd position of being able to ask questions you are never in a position to ask about a biological child," David says. "Before meeting the birth parent, you wonder if it's going to be a good match. The next day, I talked everything over with my friend, John, who was adopted. After reviewing the profiles of Megan and Andy, John said, 'There is nothing wrong with this picture. Can you think of anything bet-

Kaya Seneca Stitzhal

ter? Get a hold of yourself!' I remember at that moment feeling, 'Here we go!'"

As they contemplated meeting Megan, David and Laurel were nervous. "My dream then was just to become a parent," Laurel says. "But we gained so much more by becoming involved with Megan and Andy. At the time, I had no idea the process would become a transforming experience."

"We brought along Grateful Dead tapes for the three-hour trip from Seattle to Vancouver for our first meeting," David recalls. "We explored things to talk about. I thought we could tell Megan we used to go to Grateful Dead concerts."

"She was late for our appointment at the agency," Laurel remembers. "She arrived with grease all over her hands, because her car broke down and she had to pull over to the side of the road to fix it. She was so embarrassed, but we thought it was great."

"Eight months pregnant and she fixed her own car," David says with admiration.

As soon as Megan walked into the room, he and Laurel felt completely comfortable. "She reminded us of one of our dearest friends," David says. "Immediately, all the tension was gone." When Megan had a moment alone with the counselor, she said, "I can't believe they've been to Grateful Dead concerts!"

"The three of us went out for dinner after meeting with the counselor," David says. "Sitting across from Megan, of course we wanted to love everything about her. Although we were all supposed to sleep on our decision, we couldn't wait. As Laurel and I got into our car after dinner, we looked at each other and simultaneously said, 'She's fantastic.'"

So David leapt out and ran up to Megan's car before she pulled away. "As she rolled down the window of her little Honda Civic, I said, 'We want you to know we are psyched to move forward if you are.' In what we now know is typical Megan fashion, she responded, 'Ah, yeah.' I said, 'Cool.'"

Over the next three weeks, David and Laurel drove from their home in Seattle to Vancouver, Washington, and back many times. The three-hour trips became special times for them to be together, just the two of them, before they became parents. Together they accompanied Megan to a doctor's appointment, attended the outdoor market in Portland, visited a park with their dog Roscoe, and ate at a local fast food restaurant, Burgerville. "These places became icons to me," David says. "They are now imbued with power, like any place you go when you are falling in love."

Two weeks before the birth, he and Laurel went to dinner with Andy, Megan, Megan's little sister Kendra, Grandma Margaret (Megan's mom), Grandma Sally (Andy's mom) and Aunt Nancy (Andy's sister). "Laurel revealed a small intimacy about herself, something to welcome them all and invite them to know her," David recalls. "Margaret and Sally said in unison, 'Oh, we know that! We read and loved your whole portfolio.' We knew so little about all of them, but they knew everything about us."

On Mother's Day, Laurel and David again made the journey to visit Megan and Andy. The four of them took a long walk in one of Megan's favorite parks. At the end of the day, she revealed that the birth might be soon. Laurel and David, who were both trained doulas, felt their excitement mounting. Doula is an ancient Greek word that now refers to a labor support provider. Of all the births they would assist, this one would be the most meaningful personally.

That night, they drove back to Seattle in the pouring rain. Exhausted, they climbed into bed as soon as they got home. Then the phone rang. It was Megan. "I'm going into labor, and it's time for you to come back."

"It was one-fifteen a.m. The rain had not stopped," David recalls. "Laurel drove, since I had driven home and she had been able to get some sleep."

For the trip, Laurel had packed a necklace of her mother's which she hadn't worn for a long time, because the clasp was fragile. Her mother died when Laurel was eleven. It was important that she bring the necklace, because she needed to feel her mother was with her.

She and David arrived at the hospital at three-thirty in the morning. Laurel provided support for Megan during the labor. Kaya Seneca was born at 8:23 a.m. Margaret, Megan's mother, and David were overcome with emotion as they watched Megan deliver her baby into the world, a baby with the longest fingers and toes anyone had seen. "It was the greatest gift," David says.

The midwife knew how important it was to all of them that Kaya be placed directly on Megan's chest, but the cord got wrapped around the baby's neck during the delivery, and the midwife placed her on a nearby table to check her breathing. "I stood touching Kaya's hand, but Laurel could not leave Megan's side," David remembers. "Megan kept saying, 'Go be with her.' Kaya was only two feet away, but Laurel could not go that far. She felt her primary responsibility was to Megan. So I touched Kaya with one hand, took Laurel's with my other, and Laurel held Megan's hand."

Andy walked in less than a minute after Kaya was born. He was heartbroken to have missed his daughter's birth.

"The midwife placed Kaya in Megan's arms," Laurel remembers. "I watched as Megan lovingly held her daughter.

David, adoptive father, with Andy, birth father (Vancouver, Washington)

She just gazed at her and touched her so tenderly. I was in tears watching them together."

Then a nurse took Kaya down the hall to the nursery, where she was placed under a heat lamp for observation. Andy, David, and Laurel left Megan to be with Kaya. David remembers, "We made a circle around her bassinet and stood there staring at her. Then Andy, who is six feet two, reached in his huge hand and touched her. It hadn't even occurred to me that it was okay to touch Kaya."

With Andy and Laurel on either side, David carried Kaya back down the hall to Megan. Laurel remembers still feeling like potential parents. "Giving birth is a transforming experience. And we were prepared to support Megan's decision, even if she had a change of heart. Only she could know what was best. We trusted her completely, which allowed us to be there without fear."

During the entrustment ceremony, candles and photographs were passed around. Kaya was dressed in purple tie-dye. Megan's mother, Margaret, was there. Laurel told Megan that she would always be Kaya's first mom, that Kaya would always know that Megan loved her, and how much she had put into her life. Laurel recalls, "I had decided that I wanted to give Megan the necklace. At first it seemed too precious to give up. I couldn't imagine parting with it because it was my connection to my mother. But suddenly I understood that was exactly why the necklace was perfect. It was only too appropriate that it be something difficult to part with, something I would have to trust Megan to care for as much as I would, because of its significance.

"I put the necklace around Megan's neck, crying the whole time, and we hugged each other while Kaya was in her arms. I told her, 'I love you,' and Megan said, 'I love you, too.' I'll never forget that. Quite honestly, at that point my connection was much more with Megan than with Kaya. I had never grown so intimate with someone in such a short period of time. The beauty of our closeness was that the most wonder-

Extended family: David in center; Front row: Laurel, Megan and Andy; Back row: Andy's parents Sally and Clell, Kaya, Megan's sister Kendra, and Megan's parents Margaret and Ken

ful connection I could ever have to Kaya was through her birth mother."

David then spoke to Andy. He knew how difficult it had been for Andy to miss the birth of his daughter. David had been wearing a silver turtle earring all during labor and delivery. Megan especially loved turtles, and also wore her turtle necklace during the labor and birth. "Turtles are significant in many creation myths," David told Andy. "It is believed that their sacred power is what holds up the universe." David gave the earring to Andy. They held each other and cried.

Megan placed Kaya in Andy's arms. Andy held her for a long time, then placed her in David's arms. "During the whole ceremony, it never occurred to me to think about how the transfer would happen," David recalls. "I wasn't thinking

about Kaya that much, except in terms of her family. We were so focused on Megan and Andy. We talked about the times we would have together in the future, and about how Kaya would learn to look out the car window at the cows we had passed so many times on the drive to see them.

"We all shuffled down the hall from this sacred space, where all our lives were forever changed, and where everyone knew what was happening," David remembers. "And we burst through double doors to this public space outside the maternity ward. Out in the lobby, people were milling around. A man looked at me holding Kaya and said, 'Congratulations. Are you the Dad?' "I smiled, nodded toward Andy, and said, 'Yes, and so is he.'"

In 1963, eighteen year-old Jane Guttman left her sheltered, upper-middle-class California world and drove with her boyfriend, Mitchell, across the desert floor to Las Vegas in the heat of an August night. She was certain she was the only bride who had ever been so obviously pregnant at the altar. "I felt like I was sleepwalking," she recalls, "moving from place to place without any awareness of my next step."

Her father was shocked when he found out. He had dreamed Jane would complete college, marry someone of a similar background, and maintain respect within their community. But Mitchell was neither Jewish nor college-oriented—not the son-in-law Mr. Guttman had been hoping for.

After living for one week in a teenaged attempt at marriage, Jane returned to her father's home. His pressure and influence had prevailed, and the Las Vegas marriage was annulled. Jane was devastated. Her mother, who was separated from her father, faded from the scene, unable to cope with the enormity of the situation. Her father handled all the details of the pregnancy.

"He didn't see my child as a real person, as flesh of my flesh," says Jane. "To him, the baby was a challenge to be resolved so that my life could go on with respectability and purpose. He was a successful businessman, an executive in the theater industry, making decisions that would benefit the outer circumstances of my life. But he had no awareness of the distress and despair that would darken my inner life."

While awaiting space at St. Anne's Maternity Home in Los Angeles, Jane first stayed

Jane in the desert (Palm Springs, California)

alone in a small hotel near her home, and then moved to a more distant part of town. "My father and one of my sisters brought groceries and magazines. Television was my sole companion. As I thought about the hopelessness of my child and myself, I was filled with questions, but there was no one to ask."

When a space became available at St. Anne's, Jane's sister drove her to the home. "I felt so lost and frightened when she left me there. Everywhere I turned, I was admonished not to reveal my name or anything about myself. Shame, guilt, and sorrow permeated the place. We were not allowed to be seen in public. The nuns demanded we obey the rules. Every word or look from them was a form of punishment."

Unable to tolerate life at St. Anne's, Jane convinced her father to let her stay in the apartment of a family friend. But he insisted that she stay inside during the day, to avoid being seen by the neighbors. She was allowed to return to her father's home only after dark.

On the night of October 17, her amniotic sac ruptured. "My father picked up a stack of magazines for the anticipated wait, and we drove to St. Anne's Maternity Hospital. He was refused entry and was very upset." Labor did not begin for two days, during which time Jane was left all alone. "I did speak with my father on the phone. I assured him I was okay, but I'm certain he heard my fright and distress. I realize now that he really did care about me. He had always been a loving father. But the circumstances and the stigma trapped him. He was a victim of his shame and my impropriety."

As the moment of delivery approached, Jane was simultaneously terrified and relieved that it would all soon be over. Anticipation of the imminent separation filled her with sadness. "For two days, I listened to the sound of young mothers giving birth, to their screams of pain and suffering, and my courage faded. On October 19, at 6:10 a.m., my son was born. For days afterward, I paced up and down the hall, past the nursery. The glass that separated him from me might as well

have been a cement wall. Only the Catholic girls had the privilege of holding their babies, and then only for a few minutes while the child was baptized. I ached to hold my son. I cried all the time. The nuns walked by. Instead of offering a kind word or assurance, they reminded me that I had created this tragedy with my own behavior."

The day before her nineteenth birthday, Jane returned to her father's home. "I spent the day sleeping and crying, feeling a great emptiness, an aching, a longing. My hands rested on my flattened belly. I still sensed my son. No one wanted to hear about my sadness. The evidence had disappeared. Life would go on. From that day forward, I found fulfillment and purpose in the world, but never fully."

Now, thirty-five years later, Jane is a chiropractor and a holistic health practitioner. She lives in the desert of Palm Springs. She is also a teacher, speaker, author, and mother of another son, Josh, and a daughter, Julie. Her work, based on the belief that the body holds memories, promotes the release of traumatic cellular memory. The release is facilitated through a system of guided imagery, breathing, and Ayurvedic sound.

For thirty-five years, Jane was unable to tolerate the sound of a baby crying. If she heard it, she would have to get up and leave the room. Between August and October of every year, she repeated a cycle of pain, grief, and mourning. "For those eight weeks each year, I lived two lives: my present life and 1963."

Jane waited until the time felt right to begin the search for the son she had given up. On March 16, 1998, she posted a memo on various Internet adoption bulletin boards, stating her son's name, birth date, and place of birth. Reading message after message, she began to allow for the possibility of actually finding him. Still, she was not prepared for the magnitude of the event. The very next day, she received an e-mail with the life-changing words, 'We found him!' "I felt a lifetime of pain dissolve as I read his name, Micah, and learned where he lived. He was real. He existed.

"After I found Micah, I began piecing together the reasons for my strong reaction to babies' cries. The nursery at the maternity home was always silent, whenever I thought about it. No babies cried. I realized that for thirty-five years, I could not hear the sound of babies because I could not bear the truth of what I had allowed—that I didn't march into that nursery and take my own baby when he cried out for me. Every cry was an agonizing reminder of the tragedy of our separation."

After reviewing all the options about how to contact her son, Jane felt it best to call Micah's younger brother, Thomas. She explained who she was and asked Thomas to give her phone number to Micah. But the news was a shock, and Micah could not bring himself to call her.

From Thomas, Jane learned she is also a grandmother. That seemed to double her loss. "This is hard for my children, Josh and Julie. They don't understand how I can love Micah. How can I love him when I don't know him? Yet I love him so much. After I found him, I literally could feel him in my body as if I were pregnant again. My sister and my friends all want this pain to stop for me. They continually ask when I will get over the sorrow. Will I ever be healed? The intensity of my feelings comes from the shock that I could allow myself to release a part of me and not know the next step for him."

A few days before Micah's thirty-fifth birthday, Jane finally called him. "At the moment he answered the phone, I wanted time to stop. I wanted to hold the moment and have our first contact be endless. The call lasted twenty-five minutes. I listened to every word, holding it as the sacred gift it was. His first word, 'Hello,' was warm and melodic. At the end of the conversation, he asked for time to consider where I may or may not fit into his life. That was our only conversation. Thomas said Micah read my first letter, but has been unable to read any more. He used the word 'avalanche' to describe how it might feel for Micah to open this door."

Before calling Micah, Jane had been menstruating for days. "Strangely, after the seventeenth day of bleeding, I finally remembered the sound of my baby's cry. The nursery was no longer silent in my mind. My body kept this memory until my son's thirty-fifth birthday. I became a silent observer as my body expressed a process that demanded my attention, stopped my life, and required that I turn within to honor the place that was wounded—physically, emotionally, and spiritually. Many memories moved through my mind: motherless babies crying alone, nuns admonishing women for sins, doctors ordering sedation for both mothers and babies to numb the grief of their separation and loss. No one listened to us. No one held my son with love. Those entrusted with his care felt pity for his plight and condemnation for his mother."

On the night of Micah's thirty-fifth birthday, Jane was wheeled into the operating room for an emergency hysterectomy. "I was given an epidural block, just as I had been given one at St. Anne's for Micah's birth. Again, my arms were restrained. Only this time, I was never left alone. Loved ones were always nearby. I was 'circling the drain,' a nurse friend told me later. I knew that I might never get to meet Micah in person, that I might die.

"I feel all who have relinquished a child bear the scars of surrender. None escape without wounds, though each of us will have a greater or lesser knowledge of our pain. Even if we live our lives as if it did not happen, our cells and our souls remember.

"Each time I travel to the very depths of my sorrow, I return with the gifts of greater compassion and courage. Despite my grief, I feel released from the agony of not knowing whether Micah is safe. As expressed in the Jewish song for Passover, 'Dayenu,' just knowing he is safe is completely enough. The promise to give him life was kept. I celebrate that I gave him life. I rejoice for every gift to the world that comes from his life. I rejoice."

SUE HARRIS
and MARY NOYES

SUE HARRIS AND MARY NOYES ARE BEST FRIENDS. THEY FIT TOGETHER: ONE'S strengths are the other's weaknesses. They have been close for so many years that they can read each other's subtleties of body language and expression. Bantering back and forth, they often talk at the same time, and take turns completing each other's sentences. Their friendship became their fortress after they learned they were both adopted.

"We met in psychology class, didn't we, Mary? I think you were sitting behind me."

"In front of you," Mary says.

"There was something about you that I liked," Sue recalls. "Maybe it was how you spoke to the professor, or maybe it was hearing comments you made in class."

"You pursued me."

"I did!" Sue says, laughing. "I know I did."

"That's why I remember you in back of me," says Mary. "Every time I turned around, there you were. 'Can I have your notes? What are you doing? Are you going to the library? Did you get that book?' Because of how I reacted to being adopted, it was difficult for me to connect with other people, though I wanted to. I had friends, but I kept this wall up at the same time. Then there was Sue! I remember trying to pull away from you, but it was impossible. I was always sucked back in. I couldn't help it."

"I seduced you!"

"Yes, you seduced me. That was our sophomore year in college," Mary recalls.

Sue admired Mary's sense of responsibility. "You were working full time, going to school

Sue embracing her best friend
Mary (Milton, Massachusetts)

109

full time. You had a car. I was just a babe in the woods. Going to school was hard enough for me. I was learning to get out of bed on time in the morning to make classes."

"I never gave all I did a second thought," Mary says. "I just did it."

The year they met, Sue and Mary took a trip to Florida for spring break. "I still have a picture of you from that trip," Sue says. "You had sunglasses on. It was 8 a.m. and we had just pulled up onto the strip at Daytona Beach."

"We pulled into a Dairy Queen," Mary continues. "Somehow the topic of adoption came up. We suddenly realized we were both adopted. You were the only other adopted person I knew. We began to discover we understood and accepted each other in a way no one else could. You taught me about feelings and gave me permission to have them. You helped me to become me, to accept who I am, by loving me no matter what, without judging. I never experienced that before in a friendship."

"You were notorious for having the ugliest shoes," Sue says, laughing. "Remember those red plastic ones that didn't match anything? You were so bad with colors. We'd be in a shoe store and I would spot the ugliest shoes on the rack. I always knew they would be the only ones you'd like. I would just look at you and say, 'I don't get it!'"

"And I'd say f— you!" replies Mary with a laugh.

After graduation, Mary visited Sue's house on weekends. She'd often arrive before Sue got home from work, and spend the time talking with Sue's adoptive mother. "We mostly talked about her worries for you. You were still living at home, borrowing money from her. I couldn't believe it! I was just the opposite."

"It was painful to grow up," Sue recalls. "I remember when my mother said I had two weeks to get a job. 'Don't think you're going to move back home and I'm going to take care of you,' she said to me. I thought, 'Oh, my God! I've only got two weeks!'"

"But one funny thing I remember about you is that you

always made such a mess," Sue continues. "The minute my mother put juice and cookies out, you'd knock it all over. You'd take a bite of something and crumbs were everywhere. She still put the tablecloth on for you no matter what the mess. I'd ask her, 'Why in the world do you put the tablecloth on when you know Mary's coming?' But we both knew it was so healing for you. In your family, you couldn't spill anything without consequences. In our house, there were six kids. Spilling was no big deal."

Mary became engaged about the time Sue's mother grew ill. "At the end of her life she asked me whether I planned to buy a home. I got the impression she was hoping I would watch over you. I assured her that one of my prerequisites for choosing a husband was that he had to know you came with me."

"After my mother died, I was as close to death as you could be and still be alive," Sue says. "I don't even remember that first year."

"I have a haunting memory of that time," Mary says. Newly married, she had just moved into her new home, which was barely furnished. "It was late at night. I was sitting on the floor in the empty living room. You called, in distress. The telephone cord was stretched from the kitchen into the living room. That cord was my lifeline to you. You were so far gone that I was afraid to let go of the phone, because I might lose you. You really scared me. You didn't just lose your mother, you lost your world. Your tone of voice wasn't the same that whole year. Your face held no expression—just an emptiness."

That first year after her mother's death, Sue took warm baths all the time, because her body felt so cold. "I was grieving so many things," she remembers. "The loss of my mother—I was such a mother's girl—was piled on top of previous losses I never dealt with, the primary one being the loss of my first mother."

Her adoptive mother's death triggered Sue's search for her birth mother. "I was not looking to replace my adoptive moth-

er," she says. "But I believed finding my birth mother would give me a way to reconnect to the world and to myself." Sue went to the county courthouse to petition the judge to open her adoption file. "By some miracle the judge was able to see me immediately," she recalls. "As I sat in her chambers, she opened my records, and then spent the next hour and a half with me. I kept asking her if she was adopted, or a psychologist."

Sue saw 'Baby Girl Klayman' on the tab of her file. Her birth mother had left a letter for her, to open when Sue turned twenty-one. "I asked the judge to read it," Sue recalls. "I was too hysterical. I heard her say, 'Dear Daughter. . .' Something happened in that moment. Heat traveled through my body. She wasn't dead. She hadn't rejected me. I went straight to Mary's and called my birth mother."

At first, she didn't leave a message. "We kept calling to listen to her voice on her answering machine," Mary remem-

bers. Sue finally left a message, but she had no way of knowing that her birth mother was out of the country. As soon as she returned home, she called Sue. Sue discovered that her birth mother was highly educated and very accomplished, with a successful career. "I thought, 'Oh, my God, she's smart!'" That fact alone was a lot for Sue to absorb.

Her birth mother flew out to meet Sue right away. Mary accompanied Sue to the airport. As she approached her birth mother, Sue realized she had been expecting someone in her twenties. "I had to do a quick fast-forward. I wasn't a year old, and she wasn't twenty anymore. Now I'm in my twenties, and she's in her forties! I saw we were the exact same height and weight. We had the same lips and hands. When I saw her hand next to mine, my body became alive. I could begin to feel and understand where my body came from."

As she watched Sue and her birth mother, Mary felt alone and empty. "All of a sudden, I was the only one who didn't know where she came from," Mary recalls. "I shut down—I couldn't feel anything. I was watching their reunion from the outside looking in. I knew I was in trouble, and I didn't know what to do about it."

As soon as she got home, Mary went directly to the phone and called a therapist Sue had recommended. "At that time, I was pregnant with my first baby. I never thought I had a problem being adopted. I never thought about initiating a search. I loved my parents. But unlike Sue, I had never taken the time to tune into my feelings. When I dialed the number, it felt like I was up in the corner of the ceiling watching myself go through the motions of making the phone call. The therapist answered the phone and I said, 'My name is Mary, and I am an adoptee.'"

Mary's search was more difficult than Sue's. "When I went before the judge, I broke down crying and the judge said, 'I don't think you are emotionally ready to handle this.' Something in me snapped. I turned to him in rage and said, 'I have a right to know where I came from!' He literally threw my birth certificate at me and said, 'Good luck!' I hired a private investigator who found my birth mother in seventy-two hours. 'She's waiting for your call,' the investigator told me. Sue wasn't home. Because I wasn't able to reach her, several hours pas-

sed before I could pick up the phone. When I finally called, all I said was, 'This is the girl from Massachusetts.'"

Mary learned that her birth parents had married. She was the oldest, and the only girl of five children. "My birth father was to graduate from Virginia Military Institute on June 9th, and I was born May 29th," she says. "My birth mother told me that, in 1963, if you had a child out of wedlock, you would be kicked out of military school. So they married right after his graduation, and had four sons, each one year apart. In 1969, during a test mission, my birth father was killed when his plane exploded. A bridge in Massachusetts is named after him, Captain Thomas Burbank, as a memorial to his heroism.

"I couldn't begin to let in the pain and the sadness I felt at learning that within a few days of my surrender, my birth parents married. After hearing the story, I had conversations in my head with my father: 'If only you had decided to keep me. You may have been kicked out of military school and forced to choose a different career. But you would still be alive with all of us today.'"

"Since Sue discovered that her birth father died fairly young," Mary says, "we like to believe our birth fathers caught up with each other, and that the two of them are looking down at us, happy that we've been such great friends to each other."

JONATHAN LEE McGOWAN
(LEE, JONG SOO)

Bob and Sandy McGowan tried to turn the world upside down in order to save their son Jonathan. As it turned out, there was only one woman who could give him the chance for a new life—and it was the woman who gave him his life in the first place.

Following the the birth of their daughters, Kelly and Heather, Sandy and Bob adopted a Korean girl, Melissa (Kwak, Ok Sim) at the age of thirteen months. Two years later, in 1978, they adopted six year-old Jonathan, also from Korea. Though he was the last to arrive in the family, Jonathan changed the birth order, becoming Melissa's older brother.

During the summer between his junior and senior years of high school, Jon was attending a program at Tufts University in Boston. One night, while playing tennis with friends, he tried to jump over the net, and tripped and fell. "At first I just had small bruises on each leg," he remembers. "But within two weeks, my legs were deep purple from the knees to the toes." Initially, the McGowans weren't alarmed. When Jon came home the next weekend, they followed the advice of the Tufts health center and took him to the pediatrician. "Later that day, we received a call from the doctor asking us to bring Jonathan immediately to Massachusetts General Hospital in Boston for further testing," Sandy recalls. "Something was seriously wrong."

"We were all scared," Jon adds. "The doctors thought it was either aplastic anemia or leukemia. By early the next morning, they knew it was leukemia."

Over the next few days following the diagnosis, Jon had a blood transfusion, a blood

From left: Sandy, Bob, Jonathan, and Melissa

workup, and bone-marrow biopsy. At first doctors reassured the McGowans that ninety percent of children with leukemia go into remission with chemotherapy. After three weeks of outpatient chemotherapy and another bone marrow biopsy, they waited for the results. The news was discouraging. Jon had not gone into remission. The doctor suggested they get a second opinion. The next day they met with Dr. Yi Sheng Lee at the Dana Farber Cancer Institute in Boston. His opinion of Jon's disease was honest but hopeful. While suggesting continued chemotherapy as an inpatient at Children's Hospital to get the leukemia into remission, he also said Jon's best chance for long-term survival was to have a bone marrow transplant.

Doctor Lee explained that bone marrow contains cells that manufacture blood. In leukemia patients these cells malfunction, impeding the body's ability to produce blood and fight disease. Before a bone marrow transplant, the patient's own marrow is destroyed with radiation and chemotherapy, then replaced with disease-free donated marrow. The new marrow begins manufacturing healthy blood.

There was also frightening news. Although many children with leukemia go into remission quickly with chemotherapy, Jon had a persistent form of the disease, and it had occurred at the worst time for chances of recovery—late adolescence.

Every person's bone marrow is distinctive to them. There are literally thousands of combinations of the markers which are called tissue antigens, and a transplant requires as close a match of tissue antigens as possible. "Relatives are the most likely matches," Sandy says. "But since we didn't know Jon's birth family, the next best option was to attempt to find a donor from his ethnic group. When we called the National Bone Marrow Donor Program, we learned sobering facts: of the 208,000 registered donors, only 3,700 were of Asian descent. There was no match for our son."

Jon went through three more protocols of chemotherapy at Children's Hospital. "I spent the holidays there," he recalls.

"It was my senior year of high school. Friends visited often. Whenever my tutor came, my friends would hide in the next room and I'd pretend to be asleep, so she would leave and I could spend more time with them."

At the time they adopted Jon, Sandy and Bob learned that he had a brother, Jonas, who was one year older. Sandy wrote to the placement agency and found out that Jonas had been adopted by the Landstrom family, who lived in Sweden. "We sent them a letter with a photograph of Jonathan," Sandy says. "Apparently, the first time Jonas saw a picture of his brother, his eyes filled with tears. He said he thought they looked alike. Over the years, our families exchanged holiday cards and photos."

Twelve years later, when told about Jon's illness, Jonas volunteered to do whatever he could to save his brother's life. He flew to the United States and was reunited with Jon in the hospital. "When we first saw each other again, it was awkward," Jon remembers. "I had no idea what to say to him, and he did not know what to say to me. So, we just stared at each other." Jonas underwent blood tests, and it was discovered that his marrow was a partial match. Bone marrow transplants are risky using partial matches. The doctors were hoping for a full match. Disappointed, Jonas returned to Sweden.

After two more protocols of chemotherapy, Jon's cancer went into remission, and he was finally able to return home. He attended a total of twenty-one days of school during the remainder of his senior year.

"That summer, my father and I went to Big Sky camp in Montana, for older children with cancer," Jon says. "Against the wishes of my doctors and my mom, I rode a horse for the first time. About a month after I got home from camp, my cancer returned and I came out of remission."

It was now critical to find a bone marrow donor. The McGowan family decided to attack the problem on two fronts: to run bone marrow drives to increase Jon's possibility for a match, and to search for his birth family in Korea. "My father and my sister, Heather, then a full-time college student, were organizing bone marrow drives across the United States to try to find a donor for me," Jonathan remembers. "My dad spoke to churches and business groups, and talked on Korean radio stations in New York and Los Angeles. My sister concentrated on college organizations. I had friends at Tufts University who set up drives at their churches, and another friend set up a drive out at UCLA. My mom stayed with me as I went through more treatments at the hospital."

With the help of friends, Korean churches, and communities around the country, the McGowan family ran 175 drives, and enrolled more than 7,500 Asians in the National Bone Marrow Donor Program, raising the number of available donors in the registry to over 11,000. However, none provided a match for their son.

The family's choices narrowed. Only a few hospitals in the United States were performing mismatched transplants. The University of Kentucky at Lexington was known for its success rate. "It was a beautiful facility," Sandy recalls. During treatment, she and Jon shared an apartment near the hospital. "The staff was very upbeat. When the doctors spoke with you, they didn't ever say, 'if he makes it.' When we first visited the hospital, I asked Bob to drive me around the neighborhood so I could get a feel for it. Down the street from the hospital, I noticed a Korean church. I thought that was a good omen."

Jonas was asked to return for more comprehensive tests. His partial match might be the only chance Jon had to survive. Again, without hesitation, he boarded a plane from Sweden and joined his brother in Kentucky. The next day, Jon was scheduled to begin radiation to prepare him for the transplant. Jon, Jonas, and Sandy were in Jon's hospital room when they received the news: Jonas was not a close enough match. Bob McGowan remembers how frightened they were at the thought of Jon going through more chemotherapy. "But my son is an amazing person. By the time he'd finished the sixth round of chemotherapy, the skin on his hands and feet began to fall off. He had suffered with pancreatitis, shingles, kidney stones, and pneumonia. He had lost a lobe of one lung from a fungal infection.

"Before he entered the hospital for more chemotherapy, I remember the doctors calling me, Jon, and Sandy into a meeting. The doctors said, 'Jon, you may have heart failure or liver problems if we administer this next round of chemotherapy. Are you sure you want to go through with this?' My son quietly looked out the window, then said, 'Yes, we might as well go for it.' When Jon left the room, the doctors asked us what measures we wanted them to take to keep him alive. Did we want him placed on life support? Sandy said she would ask Jon and let them know. Driving home that same day, I was astounded by the courage I witnessed when my wife asked, 'Jon, if you're struggling to live, how much do you want the doctors to intervene with life support to keep you alive?' He thought for a while and then responded, 'Only try a little more, and then let me go, because I will have had enough. Let me go.'"

Meanwhile, a longtime friend of the McGowans, Dr. Byung Kuk Cho, who is a pediatrician from Korea, had been searching for Jon and Jonas' birth mother. Finally, Dr. Cho found her—Lee Noh Sook. "Jon and I were sitting on my bed when I told him that his birth mother, Sook, had been found," Sandy remembers. "He gave me a hug and said, 'Don't worry, you'll always be my mom.' He was letting me know no one was going to take my place in his life."

Jon's birth mother arrived in the United States in December of 1991. She was accompanied by a friend from Korea who served as her translator. Bob picked them up at the airport while Sandy and Jon waited in the apartment. "We were very anxious," Sandy recalls. "When Bob came through the door, he took me aside and said, 'Don't worry, it's going to be all right. She's a very nice woman.'"

Sook sat down beside Jon. She began to stroke his arm and

Jonathan, age 6 (Seoul, Korea)

cry. "When my birth mother walked in, it was awkward," Jon remembers. "She held my hand. Now, I'm not a person who cries in front of people, so I was staring off, not knowing what to say or do. She kept crying and saying she was so sorry. Then she said to my mother that she wasn't there to take me back. She tried to ease my mom's mind. She said she just wanted to give me another chance to live. That did help my mom."

"I think you're naturally afraid that you will lose a part of your child to the birth mother," Sandy says. "But after I met her, I wasn't worried. She did give birth to him, and due to circumstances out of her control she was unable to parent him. Jon does have two mothers."

"At one point in the hospital, Sook and Sandy were holding hands," Bob recalls. "The two mothers were sitting together, looking at Jon with such love and caring. I am so thankful

improved: four out of the six antigens matched. It was a good enough match to proceed."

Jon underwent additional chemotherapy and radiation to prepare his body for the transplant. "Just before the procedure, a nurse walked into the room with the vial holding Sook's marrow, taken from her hips a few hours earlier," Sandy recalls. "The nurse handed it to me and said, 'Guard this with your life.' I held that tiny vial and prayed."

"I was awake for the transfusion of marrow," Jon remembers. "That one vial of Sook's marrow saved my life. It was a miracle. Because it was a partial match, we weren't sure what was going to happen. But I started to improve, and after twenty-nine days in the hospital, I went back to the apartment. I had to wear a mask whenever I went outside, because I still didn't have a working immune system. The apartment was deep-cleaned every day to keep out germs. At first I was so

"HE GAVE ME A HUG AND SAID, 'DON'T WORRY, YOU'LL ALWAYS BE MY MOM.' HE WAS LETTING ME KNOW NO ONE WAS GOING TO TAKE MY PLACE IN HIS LIFE."

that Sook came forward, not only as Jon's birth mother, but also as his bone marrow donor. The procedure is totally against Korean tradition. Blood transfusions are not common there, because blood is considered a part of the soul. To give blood is to give up a part of one's soul, so she took a giant step."

"When my birth mother came to Kentucky, she stayed with friends we had made at a local Korean church," Jon says. "She came to our apartment often and prepared meals for us. She cooked one of my favorite dishes, dukpogi, which is made of skinny tubes of rice, red bean paste, onions, scallions, and sugar. I got to know her better. She went through a great deal of sadness in her life, and became a Buddhist to help her through those times. She never had any other children."

Sook's biggest fear was that she could not be the donor. "The testing took three days, and we waited anxiously to hear the results," Jon recalls. "With further testing, the match

tired, but slowly Sook's marrow began to grow in me, and I started to feel better. Now I carry Sook's blood cells, and I have her allergies. She's allergic to dairy products, so I can no longer drink milk or eat ice cream!"

The McGowans traveled to Korea in 1993 to attend Sook's wedding. "My mom said Sook would greet us at the airport with her brother, my uncle," Jon says. "When we stepped off the plane, there was a huge banner welcoming us, and a crowd of people."

Sook was married in a Buddhist temple, in a traditional Korean wedding ceremony. Jon was treated as the guest of honor by his birth mother and her new husband. And a few years later, when Jon received his college degree from Babson College in Wellesley, Massachusetts, his two mothers sat in the audience, side by side.

Sook said of Sandy, "For her I am thankful. Until I die, I will not forget."

When she was thirteen months old, Melissa came to her adoptive family from Korea carrying a little red suitcase. "My parents kept the dress I arrived in, along with my medical information and all of my papers," she says. "As I grew up, I was always able to go through these items."

After her high school graduation, Melissa made her first trip back to Korea with her family. "The flight was so long," she recalls. "I got nervous when they told us we were landing. When we touched down, it felt like I had been there before, though I wouldn't have had any recollection at all. But some part of me clicked, almost like deja vu."

Her adoptive mother, Sandy McGowan, asked Melissa if she wanted to search for her birth family while they were in Korea. "It didn't matter to me if we searched or not," Melissa says. "I was never one of those people with expectations, hoping to find information and then being crushed if they don't. I think the only real reason I wanted to find them was because of my brother's illness. Because of his need to find a relative for his bone marrow transplant, I realized the importance to adoptees of having medical information. And I was a little jealous of my brother's experience in finding his birth mother. So I said to my mom, 'Why not?'"

In Korea, they visited the Holt agency office which had orchestrated Melissa's adoption. A social worker brought out her file, which contained two reports. The first report contained the same information Melissa had grown up knowing. "You could tell she really didn't want to tell us what was in the second report," Melissa recalls. "My mother kept pressing her for more information, explaining that it was important for me to know since my brother had found his birth family. Everyone at the agency had heard about Jonathan's illness. They were all praying for him. But the woman kept saying there wasn't anything else to know. You could tell she wasn't telling the truth, that she was hesitating."

Finally, the social worker relented. The second report was the original one Melissa's birth father had signed. "That report stated that my birth parents had married, and had three other children—and that my birth mother had died. The instant I heard my birth mother was dead, I started sobbing. It almost felt like a reflex reaction, and I am usually pretty level-headed. I had no idea I would respond that way.

Little red suitcase containing Missy's X rays, medical papers, and the yellow dress and shoes worn on her journey to America.

You grow up with a certain picture in your mind of what your life was like before you came to your adoptive family. You imagine in your dreams what your parents looked like. But never in a million years did it occur to me that my birth mother might have died."

When she and Sandy left the social worker's office, Melissa's face was red and puffy, swollen from sobbing. They ran into their friend, pediatrician Dr. Byung Kuk Cho. Seeing Melissa's tears, Dr. Cho asked what happened. "I couldn't speak," Melissa recalls. "But my mom told her my birth mother had died, and said that if Dr. Cho could find out anything about her, we would really appreciate it. Though she wasn't a social worker, Dr. Cho promised to do her best. We knew it was a long shot, but Dr. Cho works miracles. She's the Korean Mother Teresa."

During the next week, Melissa, her brother Jonathan, and her parents were on the Holt Agency family tour through Korea. "I kind of forgot about everything during that week," Melissa recalls. "When we returned to Seoul, we had a message from Dr. Cho. We thought she just wanted us to go to church with her the next morning. But when my mom phoned, Dr. Cho said, 'I found Missy's birth family! Do you want to meet them? They're coming to the hotel tomorrow afternoon.'

The next morning, Melissa and her family went to church with Dr. Cho. "I was really nervous," she recalls. "We went out for lunch. When we finally went to the hotel, I started worrying about the most superficial things: am I wearing the right clothes, are they going to like me, am I going to look like them? They hadn't seen me in seventeen years. I kept walking around saying, 'I can't believe this is happening. I can't believe this is happening.' When it was time, Dr. Cho went downstairs to make absolutely certain they were my birth family."

Dr. Cho showed the family Melissa's baby picture. "Apparently, my sister said, 'I don't remember her name, and

I don't remember her birth date, but that is my sister,'" Melissa recalls. "She told Dr. Cho that she had walked with our father to the city hall, where they left me. As they were leaving, my sister turned around to look at the building, wanting to memorize the way so she could come back to get me. She saw me looking out the window at her. She never forgot seeing the top portion of my face framed in that window."

Melissa waited with her parents, so nervous she was afraid to breathe. Dr. Cho was the first through the door. "My heart was pounding," she recalls. "Then my birth family entered, bowed, and greeted my parents. Dr. Cho introduced them: my oldest brother, my sister, her daughter." Everyone sat down, and Melissa's sister started sobbing. "She was feeling so much," Melissa remembers. "She sat on the bed next to me and patted my head, patted my hand. It was as if she were touching me to see if I were real. Everything was coming back to her."

Through the translator, they learned that for months before Melissa was born, her mother was complaining of frequent headaches. Seven months after Melissa's birth, she died. "The family tried to keep me for a little bit," Melissa explains. "But they didn't have enough food. My sister would put me on her back and take me around to the other homes, trying to get the mothers to feed me. She'd say, 'Oh, my sister is really hungry, can you feed her?' The women would say, 'No,' because they didn't have anything. My sister was seven years old."

When her sister found out Melissa was in Korea, there was only one bus that she could catch to make the reunion. Korean custom treated such events as forgotten parts of history, not to be discussed, so she had never told her husband about her youngest sister. She worried that her husband and his family would reject that part of her. But when she told him the whole story, he said, "Of course you have to go. I'll watch the kids. You just get on that bus right now."

Missy's birth mother at age 18 with her nephews (Mokpo, Korea)

Melissa's second oldest brother was delayed in getting to the reunion by an auto accident. Her oldest brother blinked back tears as he looked at her. "I'd seen my brother Jonathan do that same thing," she reflects. "They all kept saying that they felt so guilty that I was the only one who had to go overseas. Growing up, they had read a lot of negative propaganda against international adoptions, and wondered what had happened to me. My parents kept saying, 'We are so thankful. Your father made the right choice. He allowed Melissa to be part of our family.' Because family is so important in Korea, I wouldn't have had much of a chance. A motherless child is not looked at well. That's why my brothers and sister had a hard life, especially after my father left them."

Melissa's oldest brother kept saying, "She looks like the other brother, the other brother."

"When my second brother arrived, I thought 'I don't look like him. I look like the other two,'" Melissa says. "Now I can see

121

that my second brother and I have the same facial expression."

Getting to know each other took a while because everything needed to be translated. "My sister would talk for twenty minutes and the translator would repeat what she had said with two English words," recalls Melissa. "A lot of the time was spent just looking at each other."

Whereas the first visit to Korea was sad, with everyone crying, the second visit was much happier. "The first time we met, Dr. Cho had suggested I greet my birth family American style, with a hug, which I did. Since their custom is to bow, they were all a little uncomfortable with my hugs that first time," she says. "On our second visit two years later, my sister hugged me, which was a huge thing given their culture."

Melissa discovered that her grandmother was still alive and wanted very much to meet her. Her adoptive mother and sister Heather accompanied her on that visit. "I walked up the stairs to her house and took off my shoes when I entered," Melissa says. "I was trying to be very polite. I had asked my Korean friends at school what would be the most respectful thing to say to my grandmother when we first met. They taught me to say in Korean, 'It's very nice to meet you.' My grandmother was totally impressed. She took my hand and patted it, and then started crying. I couldn't understand anything she was saying. We all sat on the floor. My niece was on my lap and my grandmother was right next to me, just looking at me and holding my hand. She was so cute, just this tiny little woman. I didn't want to look, but she was staring. So I looked at her and smiled, and she just chuckled."

Meeting her grandmother and her uncle, her father's brother, created a stronger connection to her birth parents for Melissa. "My uncle praised my father," she says. "My grandmother, who took care of me after my mother died, kept saying, 'I failed you. I'm so sorry I failed you. I told your father not to do it, but he didn't listen to his mother.'"

Melissa can understand her father's need to leave his family behind. "The stress of losing your wife, then relinquishing your child and having your oldest son run away all at once must have been too much to handle. Growing up, the number of times I thought about my birth father couldn't compare to the number of times I thought about my birth mother. Maybe it's because she carried me. But when I think about everything now, all the decisions that have profoundly affected my life were made by him. I wouldn't have come to America if he hadn't relinquished me. When he took me to the city hall, he said he wanted his daughter to go overseas so she would have a better chance."

The second time she visited them, Melissa observed that her brothers and sister were closer to one another than they had been during her first visit. "My second brother had stopped going to church. But once they found me, he said his faith in God was restored, and he is going to church again. My sister writes me letters saying that I am the hope of the whole family. It sometimes feels like so much pressure, and I feel guilty for not doing enough. We are family, but our cultures and environments are so different. I never feel so American as when I walk down the streets in Korea. Even the way Americans carry themselves is so different.

"I can honestly say that I think of my birth family every day, and I worry about them. Some of my friends speak fluent Korean, so I have them call my family to let them know how I am doing. When they put me on the phone with my sister, I don't know what to say. My friends reassure me—they say she just wants to hear my voice."

SHARON JINKERSON

SHARON JINKERSON WAS ONE OF THE THOUSANDS OF FIRST NATION CHIL-
dren taken from their mothers during the Fifties and Sixties 'scoop' of aboriginal children.
These children were moved from one home to another in an effort to prevent their foster parents from becoming too attached. From the age of six months until she was two
years old, Sharon was placed in sixteen foster homes.

When approached by the social worker at their church about taking one of the many
Indian children, the Jinkersons felt their time for having babies had passed. Their
youngest son was four. But they couldn't bear the thought of a child without a home, so
they agreed to take two year-old Sharon for a couple of weeks.

They would soon have a change of heart. "My adoptive mother said she fell in love
with me immediately," Sharon relates. "She tells me, 'We didn't even get your bags
unpacked and I knew you belonged to us. I knew we weren't going to let you go.'"
Sharon's experience in the foster care system had left its scars. By the time she arrived
in her adoptive family's Vancouver home, she was developmentally delayed and terrified
of people.

At the time of her placement, the social worker had advised the Jinkersons that
telling Sharon about her heritage might create low self-esteem, and that it should remain
a secret. But growing up, Sharon's darker skin and exotic facial features made her stand
out. Her adoptive family all had blond hair and blue eyes. During the summer, Sharon's
skin turned practically black in the sun, and remained that way for months. When she

123

returned to school in September, she was always teased about being a half-breed. "I felt so ashamed and helpless," she remembers. "Children pulled my hair and lifted my dress and called me 'squaw.' A part of me began to believe that what they teased about was true. Maybe I was a squaw. I wondered what my parents would think if they knew. I was a small child, trying to figure this out all alone."

Although Sharon's parents never spoke in depth about her background, they wanted her to have a positive view of her First Nations' culture, so they took her to museums and showed her the Indian beadwork and baskets. "I would get a huge lump in my throat, and I could hardly wait to get out. I would be the first one back in the car," she recalls. "Sometimes I'd even wait in the car while they were still going through the museum. As an adult, I see that the experience was like looking at pictures of a family who I thought didn't want me. My mother eventually decided that I had no interest in that culture and stopped taking me to museums displaying indian art."

When Sharon was fifteen, her favorite cousin handed her the book *Seven Arrows*. "When I asked her why she thought I should read it, she said it was about 'my people.' I put it back on her shelf and told her I had to go home." Her cousin's words filled Sharon with excitement and confusion. "There was no other way I could take her words. I was native. What I had always known inside was real. It was the first total acknowledgment of my aboriginal background. I ran home, with my heart pounding. I ran into the house feeling this huge energy. I ran up to my room, slammed the door, and laid across my bed, angry and confused.

"Finally, I went out to the kitchen and asked my mother why I wasn't adopted until I was seven years old. I wasn't going to let her off the hook with my questions anymore. She got her coffee and sat down, nervous as usual about this subject. 'Actually, your mother never signed the adoption papers for consent,' she explained. 'So it took that long to process.'

'Did you see my mom in court?' 'Well, yes.' 'Was she native?' I asked. Struggling, my mother answered, 'Well, maybe a bit.'"

In her mid-twenties, Sharon lived on Beach Avenue in Vancouver. She drove a yellow Volkswagen named Buttercup, and was studying to be a teacher. "On the surface I guess I looked like your average person," she reflects. "But deep down inside I was unhappy, and felt an emptiness I did not understand. Life didn't seem to have much meaning. Sometimes I had the feeling I was running and something was trying to catch up with me. My dreams seemed so real, I feared I wouldn't come back from them.

"I saw a psychiatrist and in time, after getting to know me, he said, 'Your problem doesn't lie in your present or your future.' I was twenty-six years old and he was the first one who said, 'You need to search for your original family. Your solution is in your past.'

"In the summer of 1985, I wrote to the Canadian government for information about my adoption. I was on the phone with my friend Elaine, an anthropologist and the curator of the Museum of North British Columbia, when the mailman arrived with a letter from Victoria. I had completely forgotten about sending for my information, and was joking about getting a parking ticket when I read the letterhead, 'Adoption Division.' I remember feeling very emotional. 'It says my grandparents were both aboriginal, my great-grandparents and great-great-grandparents were all aboriginal.' Elaine screamed, 'Sharon, your mother is full native! You may be a member of a band!' I kept saying, 'My mother is native. She isn't a quarter native, a part native, or maybe native—she IS native!'"

The next morning, Sharon called the Department of Indian Affairs, and made an appointment with a department representative, Peggy, at 11:30 that same day. Sitting on a bus on the way to meet with Peggy, holding the letter in her hand, Sharon caught her reflection in the window. "I don't know who you are," she thought.

Sharon (right) and Auntie Grace on the Key Reserve (Canora, Saskatchewan)

"Peggy stared at the papers holding my non-identifying information. She said, 'We have a person working for the Department of Indian Affairs who is willing to give out secret information to native adoptees who want to know if they are treaty status.' She made the phone call to Ottawa. When she hung up, she looked at me and said, 'You are an Ojibiway Indian. You have treaty status.'

"Weeks later, I received a phone call at home," Sharon recalls. "I could hear only breathing at the other end. I was just about to hang up when I heard, 'This is Rebecca talking to you.' I said, 'Rebecca?' 'Your grandmother. I'm coming to visit you.' My grandmother? Totally numb, I got out my calendar. When I asked her when she would like to come, my granny said, 'Oh, I'll be there soon.' 'Soon' turned out to be a few weeks later, in December of 1986.

"By that time, I had met Victor, now my husband, who is a full native and a member of the Tsimpshian Tribe, 'People of the River Mist.' He encouraged me by saying, 'You have a place with your people. They will remember you. They wonder where that little girl is.'"

It was her grandmother's daughters, Auntie Grace and Edna, who brought Sharon home to the Key Reserve for the first time. Sharon's return was celebrated with ceremony and great joy. Her grandmother, a traditional elder, gave thanks to the creator for the return of her grandchild, and for the fact that Sharon's family had been so kind to her while she was growing up.

"Everyone was fighting over me: 'I'm the one taking Sharon up to see the new stop sign!' 'No, I am!' At one point, I was sitting at Granny's table in my skirt and patent leather shoes, sipping tea, when one of my cousins came in carrying a broomstick with sixteen rabbits strung on it. They were to be prepared for a traditional feast. I screamed. The only hunting I had ever done was at Safeway. My Uncle Sterling just looked at me and said, 'Grab a knife.'

"My aunties argued over who was going to sleep with me. Granny won the argument. That night, she tucked me into bed, then crawled in beside me. She kept me up until sunrise, telling stories."

Sharon believes her grandmother transformed her life by

sharing the traditions of the Ojibiway people. Over the next seven years, she began to know her own spirit because of Granny's love, kindness, and patience. "The lessons sometimes came from formal instruction and sometimes casually, like when we'd be standing in line at Wal-Mart and suddenly Granny would get a little inspiration and begin to share some amazing information. I could never predict when the teachings would come. That was her magic!

The times with my Gran were when I felt the most alive, because she encouraged me to express and trust my true self. I was becoming whole through the rituals and rites of passage that my people have practiced for thousands of years. I was beginning to feel a sense of belonging that I had never experienced. I like to say I was 're-belonged' to myself and my people. This is my medicine."

Sharon studied the traditional teachings with her grandmother for seven years. They began doing sacred pipe ceremonies together, re-enacting the creation of all life. "My Granny told me to look up inside the stem of her pipe. 'The curve of the pipe symbolizes your life path,' Gran whispered as I looked up through the hole. 'You can see the light at the end of the stem. That is your journey—to the light,' she said. 'At the end of your journey, the pipe will go to someone else, and they will walk the same path up the stem of your pipe.'"

Granny had learned the teachings from elders who were alive before her band had been contacted by the missionaries. She understood that in order for their culture to be preserved, it had to be shared. Sharon, she felt, would be able to bridge both cultures. So Granny prepared her to carry her 'medicine bundle,' and gave her the name White Thunder Woman. "Now you walk the earth," she said.

'If I had been raised in the Ojibiway culture, I would have been given my name when I was two years old," Sharon explains. "The belief is that the baby lingers in the 'moss bag,' the place between the spirit world and the earth, until the age

of two. I was twenty-eight. She told me my medicine would be thunder. 'It's a good thing to put out tobacco every time you hear the thunder,' Gran said, 'to thank the creator for your name.'"

When her grandmother's health declined, Auntie Grace took care of her. Sharon felt too terrified to deal with the reality that her wise and gentle elder would soon leave this world. Even when Granny was taken to the hospital, Sharon couldn't bring herself to visit. "I could feel my grandmother pulling me to her. I said to her spirit, 'I'm not ready to say goodbye to you.'"

She and Victor joined a group of friends who were taking a traditional Northwest coast canoe out on the ocean. "We brought our son Solomon with us. The sun was setting as we paddled the canoe back home. All of a sudden, I felt a huge wave of emotion come over me. Now, I never drum or sing. My voice would throw the Mormon Tabernacle Choir off-key. But I suddenly stood up, as if I was being lifted out of the canoe, and I pounded Victor's drum and sang the only honor song I knew. I've heard many elders describe the passage to the spirit world like a canoe moving from the shore of this world to the shore of the spirit world. The deceased looks back at this world from the canoe and sees loved ones.

"Victor asked what happened to me, and I didn't know. But as we drove home, I knew Granny had passed over."

The phone was ringing when they pulled into the driveway. "Victor ran to answer it. I was getting Sol out of his baby seat. Victor came back out and I knew by the look on his face. He said, 'She passed away twenty minutes ago.'"

But her granny's spirit did not leave. "When we arrived at the hospital, her spirit was still there in the room," Sharon remembers. "My Auntie Grace said, 'Your Granny's been waiting for you.' And I told them, 'I just couldn't come.' I spoke to her spirit. 'Granny, go. I'm here with you now. It's okay. I'll never forget you.' I felt I was on a train platform. She was pulling away and I couldn't stop the train. As the train pulled further and further away, I waved like I was a little girl, and watched her go."

I would like to express my love and gratitude to those who have supported me in my life. To my adoptive mother, Ruth Osler, for your consistent belief in me—I miss you; to my Uncle George, for your wide open arms and big, inviting belly; to Zelda Shuwall, for your love as a mother and your zest for life; to Buz Teacher, for providing me with the opportunity to write this book, for your continued friendship and the manner in which you father our son; to Janet Teacher, for offering an open ear and heart to Matthew; to Wayne Bliss, for meeting me when you were twenty–five, and loving me as a sister; to Herb Rappaport, for broadening my view of the world and myself; to Dennis O'Hara, for showing me what it looks like to be a gentle and sharply insightful therapist; and to Douglas Eli Cox, for the way you live your life—you are an inspiration to me.

To my women friends: to Gail Potamkin Faulkner, for childhood memories of crumbled hamburger and squeezed bodies in a twin bed; to Leslie Tuttle, my partner in crime through graduate school, for all the laughter that helped get us through; to Lynne Herman, my 'sister', for sharing everything in my life; to Ann Alburn, for good times with our children and your help up the spiral stairs of the Statue of Liberty; to Reva Rohlfs, for your warm and loving heart; to Neil Allen, for our morning coffee talks and for keeping order in my life; to Penny Partridge, for patiently listening until I figured out what I had to say. And to Niki Berg, for your example of openness and courage.

To my family—Taffy, Jeff, Rebecca, Hannah, Daniel, Susie, Michael, Jeff and Val—for your love.

Finally, to my husband, Rich, for your tender, nurturing, healing soul. And a hot, homemade meal, always ready.

—MAK

My heartfelt thanks to my mother and father for birthing me; to my siblings, Stephen, Allan, and Judy, for being such an important part of my history; to my sons–in–law, Jim and Joe, and my grandchildren, Rachel, David, and Daniel, for your love and trust.

To Dave King, for your generous help; to Carla Shapiro, for your artistic eye; to Emily Gwathmey, for your talented editing; to Annabel Zall, for keeping me organized; to Jane Goldberg, for your brilliant insights; to my labs, the Edge, and Mark Markheim, for your outstanding work; to Judith Stitzal, Renee Goldman, and Peter Matson, for your expert guidance; to Diane Cook, Len Jenshel, Charles Brooks, Barbara and Arnold Beckerman, Neil Beckerman, Robert Dow, and Cynthia and Richard Babat, for your ongoing help and support; and to Mary Ann, your kindness of spirit and sense of humor make you a remarkable partner and friend.

Lastly, to my husband, Peter, for your unwavering devotion and continuous encouragement throughout our long partnership. I cannot imagine life without you.

—NB

Our heartfelt gratitude to our friends: Sondra Howell, who first suggested that we might make a good team; to Pam Hasegawa, for your knowledge and enthusiasm about this project; and a special thanks to Carol Schaefer, who received stories in the rough and returned each one beautifully sanded and polished.

Our sincere appreciation to everyone at Running Press who contributed to this project. Our deepest thanks to Jason Rekulak, our editor at Running Press, for your skill with words, guidance, wicked sense of humor, and apparent calm while maintaining a vision of the finished book. And to Mary Ann Liquori, for creating a beautiful, classic design and for your abundance of patience and ability to hear us.

—MAK & NB